No Doubt:
The Murder(s) of
Oscar Grant

Thandisizwe Chimurenga

No Doubt:
The Murder(s) of
Oscar Grant

Thandisizwe Chimurenga

Ida B. Wells Institute | Los Angeles, CA

323 . 283 . 9016 | www.triplemurder.com

info@triplemurder.com

No Doubt: The Murder(s) of Oscar Grant

The Ida B. Wells Institute

Los Angeles, CA

Copyright 2014 Thandisizwe Chimurenga

Printed in the United States of America | subjugated NuAfrika

Library of Congress Cataloging-in-Publication Data:

Criminal Justice – Media Criticism – Black/Ethnic Studies

Chimurenga, Thandisizwe – No Doubt: The Murder(s) of Oscar Grant

ISBN 978-1489596291

Published by the Ida B. Wells Institute

Cover design by Myshell Tabu. Cover Photo: Francisco Alvarez at the Los Angeles County Superior Court, taken on the author's cell phone. Back Cover Photo: Oscar Grant, courtesy of the Johnson Family.

Excerpt from "Poem About Police Violence," by June Jordan from *Directed by Desire. The Collected Poems of June Jordan,* Copyright 2005 June Jordan Literary Estate Trust; reprinted by permission. www.junejordan.com

TABLE OF CONTENTS

PREFACE

"If you are silent about your pain, they'll kill you and say you enjoyed it."

~Zora Neale Hurston

He was on his stomach. Prone. Trying to breathe, with a cop's knee pressing on his head. And then he was shot in the back. That was a few minutes after 2:00 a.m. on January 1, 2009. He would die from that gunshot wound about seven hours later. His name was Oscar Grant and Johannes Mehserle, at the time a Bay Area Rapid Transit Authority (BART) police officer, would stand trial for Grant's murder from June 10 until July 8, 2010, in Los Angeles, CA. Mehserle would be found guilty of Involuntary Manslaughter and, although he was sentenced to two years in state prison, he would serve his time in the Los Angeles County Jail and leave in June, 2011 under the cover of darkness.

I covered the trial of Johannes Mehserle for Oscar Grant's murder for several Bay Area news outlets, attending every day except for two. In this book I argue that both Johannes Mehserle and Anthony "Tony" Pirone murdered Oscar Grant as a result of white supremacy: the "power structure of formal or informal rule, socioeconomic privilege, and norms for the differential distribution of material wealth and opportunities, benefits and burdens, rights and duties" that privileges people of Caucasian - European descent.

This book is many things: it is an absolute

repudiation of Mehserle's defense argument that he meant to pull his taser and not his automatic weapon on the morning that he murdered Grant; it is a critique of many aspects of how the media handled this case; it is a critique of how the judicial system worked in this case, as well as the judicial system's insistence that Grant was not murdered since 12 jurors said he wasn't.

This book is also a look at the phenomenon of state-sanctioned violence in the form of police murder, and how that phenomenon operates with impunity in the United States of America. Police murder violently rips Black and Brown people, young men in particular, from our families and our communities; this book provides a look at this phenomenon through the lens of this one particular case. In this work I define state-sanctioned violence as the physical, coercive and deadly force committed by and on behalf of a government through its enforcers – the police – against Afrikan-descendant people.

But mostly, this work is my witnessing. I knew just before the start of the trial that I would be writing this book but that was all I knew. The journey to write this book was plagued with internal sabotage: I didn't know if I was up to the task; I didn't know how I would pay my bills when I needed time to write the book; I didn't know if anybody would read the book; I didn't know if I should put the book down and move on to something else; I didn't know who I thought I was that I could write the book. I didn't know a lot of things.

Fortunately, in the end, it really wasn't up to me. The book is written and the book is here because it needs to be here. And that's all I need to know.

Here is what you need to know: I have relied on the actual words of witnesses and the defendant in this case and not simply my own recollections. The reason for this is because both the defendant and the witnesses in this case were told to raise their hands and swear an oath to tell the truth, the whole truth, and nothing but, before their testimony could begin. Of course that's no guarantee that a person will actually tell the truth however, there is this little thing called 'perjury' that does exist. If it can be proved that a person lied after taking this oath the punishment is jail time. *That* is supposed to mean something; *that* is supposed to mean that this thing that is about to be embarked upon, commonly called a criminal trial, is serious business and should be respected. This book is one attempt to see how true that is.

Chapter One retells what happened on the Fruitvale BART Station platform on the morning of January 1, 2009. It is told via both the use of witness testimony and descriptions of video recordings entered into evidence in this trial.

Chapter Two retells the lies that were told via Johannes Mehserle's defense team in an effort to shield him from the responsibility of causing Oscar Grant's death, along with the other man responsible for the murder of Oscar Grant, Anthony Pirone. The second murder of Oscar Grant begins in the lies told in court and in legal documents.

Chapter Three is my analysis of how media engaged in the third murder Oscar Grant. I have included screenshots of commentary on Oscar's death from a total of four sources though many, many others were out there. These sources were most readily available for all to see in that there were no passwords required and no privacy settings were broached; one of the sources even came to me via a Google Alert system I set up with Oscar Grant's name.

The reason I included these screenshots is to illuminate how such commentary – reactionary, vile, vicious, and white supremacist at its core – serves as echo chamber and cheerleader for not only state-sanctioned violence against Afrikan people, but as moral and tangible support for and blind acceptance of more repressive and ever-increasing police powers, budgets, militarization, policies, practices, procedures, and zero accountability for police behavior that results in the murder(s) of Oscar Grants and others.

Chapter Four looks at manslaughter and murder, the charges that Mehserle was faced with, and the actual charge he should have faced if the U.S. were not a white supremacist state.

Chapter Five shows the ways in which Johannes Mehserle's murder of Oscar Grant follows the playbook of police murders in particular (and white supremacist murder in general) across the country, from Trayvon Martin to Ramarley Graham to Kenneth Harding and so, so, so many others.

Chapter Six reiterates a definition of white supremacy as well as my explication of it and state-sanctioned violence historically, and the Afterword provides my thoughts on how we can check this phenomenon.

LIST OF KEY INDIVIDUALS

Oscar Julius Grant, III, murder victim
Sophina Mesa, fiancé of Oscar Grant
Jackie Bryson, friend of Oscar Grant
Nigel Bryson,   "   "
Michael Greer,   "   "
Johntue Caldwell,   "   "
Carlos Reyes,   "   "
Fernando Anicette   "   "
Jamil Dewar,   "   "
Chris Rafferty,   "   "
David Horowitch, BART Passenger
Agnes Zafiratos, BART Passenger/Witness
Dennis Zafiratos, BART Passenger/Witness
Keecha Williams, BART Train Operator
Pamela Caneva, BART Passenger/Witness
Daniel Liu, BART Passenger/videotape witness
Karina Vargas, BART Passenger/videotape witness
Tommy Cross, BART Passenger/videotape witness
Margarita Carazo, BART Passenger/videotape witness

Cops
Anthony "Tony" Pirone, BART PD
Marisol Domenici, BART PD
Johannes Mehserle, BART PD
Jon Woffinden, BART PD
Jonathan Guerra, BART PD
Emery Knudtson, BART PD
Terry Foreman, BART PD
Alex Hidas, San Leandro PD
Greg Meyer, Use of Force expert
Don Cameron, Use of Force expert
Peace Officers Research Association of California

Courts

Judge C. Don Clay	Judge Morris Jacobson
Tom Orloff	Nancy O'Malley
David Stein	David E. Mastagni
Michael Rains	John Russo
John Burris	Judge Robert Perry

Abridged Timeline of Events

January 1, 2009
Johannes Mehserle shoots Oscar Juliuss Grant, III in the back on the Fruitvale BART Rail Station Platform; Grant is pronounced dead at Highland Hospital around 9 a.m.

January 2
KTVU airs cell phone video of Fruitvale BART shooting; Oscar is identified by name, Mehserle is not; Grant family hires attorney John Burris

January 3
First video of Fruitvale shooting appears on YouTube

January 5
Mehserle misses his first meeting with BART internal affairs investigators; reschedules for January 7

January 6
San Francisco Chronicle suggests Mehserle may have been going for his taser instead of his gun; John Burris files initial claim against BART

January 7
Funeral of Oscar Grant is held in Hayward, CA; first mass protest over Oscar's murder; protesters rebel, 105 arrests are made; Mehserle's lawyer and union representative attend BART Internal Affairs meeting and tender his resignation via letter.

January 12
Warrant for the arrest of Johannes Mehserle is signed

January 14
Mehserle is booked into the Santa Rita County Jail on the charge of murder; he was apprehended in Nevada where he had fled, according to his attorney, due to death threats against his family.

January 30
Contents of Mehserle's bail motion made public; bail is granted in the amount of $3 million dollars;

February 6
Mehserle is released on bail

May 18
Mehserle preliminary hearing begins

June 4
Preliminary hearing concludes; Mehserle ordered to stand trial

September 4
Hearing held to dismiss charges against Mehserle based on

preliminary hearing judge's "improper conduct"
September 10
Court denies Mehserle's motion to dismiss
September 11
Defense files motion requesting change of venue
October 16
Change of venue is granted; Mehserle's trial ordered out of Alameda County
November 19
Los Angeles is chosen for Mehserle's trial
January 8, 2010
Demonstration at first pre-trial hearing in Los Angeles
February 19
2nd Los Angeles pre-trial hearing; protest held in New York in solidarity
May 7, 2010
3rd and final Los Angeles pre-trial hearing
June 8
Trial begins with jury selections and remaining motions; hundreds rally in front of courthouse.
July 1
Jury begins deliberations
July 8
Mehserle convicted of Involuntary Manslaughter and immediately taken into custody; Demonstrations are held in several cities
November 4
KTVU television station airs jailhouse interview with Mehserle; protestors denounce the station
November 5
Mehserle is sentenced to two years in state prison
Jun 13, 2011
Johannes Mehserle is released from Los Angeles County Jail
May 9, 2012
Mehserle appeals his conviction for Involuntary Manslaughter
June 8
Mehserle's conviction upheld by California State Appellate Court
September 12, 2012
California State Supreme Court refuses to hear Mehserle's appeal

Bay Area Rapid Transit System map: (1) The Embarcadero is where the New Year's Eve fireworks celebration was/is held; (2) West Oakland Station where a man with a gun was apprehended earlier in the evening; (3) Fruitvale Station where Oscar Grant was murdered; (4) Hayward, Oscar Grant's destination. BART Map for developers, licensed under the **Creative Commons** Attribution-Share Alike 3.0 Unported license.

CHAPTER ONE

Truths and Damn Truths

"There's no doubt in my mind that Mr. Mehserle intended to shoot Oscar Grant with a gun and not a Taser."
~Honorable C. Don Clay, June 4, 2009

"Don't be out there drinking and driving; take the BART," she said.

Wanda Johnson didn't want anything to happen to her youngest son Oscar Julius Grant, III and his friends. It was December 31, 2008, and Oscar, his fiancé Sophina Mesa and their friends Michael Greer; Carlos Reyes; Jackie Bryson and his younger brother Nigel; Johntue Caldwell; Jamil Dewar; Chris Rafferty and Fernando Anicette were going to ring in the New Year watching fireworks with more than 200,000 other folks at the Embarcadero, San Francisco's waterfront. The fireworks are launched from barges floating out in San Francisco Bay, one thousand feet or so away from the pier. Although the display is less than 30 minutes and usually over by midnight various shops and businesses remain open, especially the city's bars and night clubs, allowing New Year's Eve revelers to enjoy themselves for several hours.

"Okay mom," Oscar told her. "I'll take BART, just because you asked." That was around 8 p.m.

It was Wanda's birthday and Oscar and Sophina, their four-year old daughter Tatiana had been celebrating at Wanda's home with a fish fry and gumbo along with other family members. Their plan was to drop Tatiana off with Sophina's sister and then meet up with friends before heading into San Francisco to the waterfront. Instead, they decided the group would meet at the Hayward Bay Area Rapid Transit (BART) Train Station and ride into the city.

The ride into the city at around 11:30 was boisterous but uneventful. Unfortunately, the group had missed the fireworks display by the time they reached the Embarcadero. Joining with the throngs of other New Year's Eve celebrants, they walked round the pier and other parts of the city before catching a train back across the San Francisco Bay. The ride back however would not be as uneventful as the one into San Francisco.

It was a "crush load." That's the term that BART uses for rail cars that have more than 200 passengers. On New Year's Day, 2009, all eight of the cars comprising the train leaving San Francisco's waterfront heading southeast through Oakland were filled to capacity, if not beyond. As it pulled into Oakland's Fruitvale Station at 1:59 a.m., the New Year's revelers, traveling towards Dublin, were packed into the aisles and some passengers were even pressed against the train doors.

At some point, between the Lake Merritt station in downtown Oakland and Fruitvale in the Southeast portion of the city, an "altercation" took place. Described by some passengers as a "scuffle," the incident caused enough concern that Agnes Zafiratos, sitting with her husband Dennis, used the intercom system to call the operator, Keecha Williams, telling her "there's a fight on the train."

The "fight" was on the lead or first car – Williams' car – but when she looked through her window into the body of the train she wasn't able to see anything since passengers were pressed up against the glass. Once the train's doors opened the altercation "spilled out" onto the platform as train riders exited.

A second call had come through on the intercom; this time it was Dennis Zafiratos. Williams asked him if he could describe the people who were involved. "A group of Black males. No weapons." That's what Zafiratos told Williams and that's what Williams relayed to BART dispatch as she had been instructed to do. She was told to "hold" the train at the Fruitvale Station until a police officer could respond. By the time Mehserle's trial came to Los Angeles, various witnesses had stated that the "altercation" that had taken place on the train involved a man named David Horowitch who was with his son; and Oscar Grant, as well as several of his friends who were with him. When the train doors opened at Fruitvale, witnesses had also testified that Sophina Mesa was arguing, saying something to someone still on the train as she and the others exited. The group stood on the platform and talked amongst themselves. They could either re-board the train or wait for another. "Popo coming?" Keecha Williams said Nigel Bryson asked her. She nodded her head yes, and Bryson said the group should leave rather than wait for another train.

Perhaps Bryson knew that he and his friends would be blamed for the incident. Witnesses would state that the altercation involved Blacks, whites and Latinos, but Zafiratos' call to the conductor only stated Black males. Jackie Bryson and Michael Greer lived about a mile or so from the Fruitvale station. The group decided that would be their destination.

From there they could either catch a ride back to the Hayward train station, about 20 or so miles south of Oakland, or they could spend the night at the apartment and take off at sunrise.

Caldwell, Dewar, Mesa and Anicette walked ahead of the group, making their way downstairs. Before the others could join them however, Officer Anthony Pirone, a former United States Marine police officer who had been with BART for four years, had made his way upstairs. He and his partner Marisol Domenici, a BART police officer for four and a half years, had been in the process of arresting a drunk and disorderly New Year's reveler at the street level entrance to the train station. The call from dispatch said there was "a 242 on a train," the California Penal Code for battery, involving a "large group of BMs, all black clothing." Both Oscar and Jackie were wearing dark colored t-shirts; Michael, Nigel and Carlos were wearing black/dark blue jackets and Pirone headed straight for them once he arrived upstairs.

Johntue Caldwell, Sophina Mesa, Fernando Anicette, Jamil Dewar and Chris Rafferty traveled along the platform and downstairs to the main entrance. Oscar and Michael Greer had gotten back onto the train while Reyes and the Brysons kept walking but they only made it a few feet before they were stopped in their tracks by Pirone who told them to "have a seat" against the station wall. The trio complied with the officer's request but Pirone, who had seen two Black males with black/dark clothing get back onto the train, may have felt personally slighted by the duo's actions.

"'Shut the fuck up.' I guess one of the kids said something to him," said Pamela Caneva, one of the

BART passengers that New Year's morning. She was referring to Reyes, Jackie or Nigel Bryson, the trio that Pirone had sitting against the wall.

"And then I guess maybe another kid said something [to Pirone] and he said, he yells again, he yells, 'I don't wanna hear a fuckin' word out of your mouth.' So I think he was pretty angry."

Before leaving the trio by the wall Pirone had radioed for Domenici to assist him upstairs. Once she made it to the platform he directed her to watch the three young men while he returned to the train to get the other two Black males. The three young men were seated against the back wall of the platform across from what can be considered the mid-way point of the eight-passenger train.

Once Domenici made it to the requested location Pirone walked angrily along the platform next to the train, heading up towards the first or lead car, looking into the windows, and using his taser to point at both Oscar Grant and Michael Greer.

" … He just kept yelling, 'Get the fuck off my train. Get the fuck off my train,' " said Caneva.

Karina Vargas was so taken aback by Pirone's behavior that she took out her video camera to record the scene unfolding before her eyes. ",,, [W]hen they were banging on the train … they were using foul language, so that's really my reason why I started recording," she stated.

A total of four videos taken by BART riders that New Year's morning were entered into evidence in court. Video but no audio from a BART surveillance camera was also entered. The videos were played, sometimes via slow motion, on a large screen television and a red laser pointer was provided to the witnesses who videotaped.

"He was yelling, and he repeatedly kept saying to the boys to 'get the fuck off the train' ... first, he was banging on the windows of the car while he was saying it, and he was pointing. So it looked like he was pointing at the people that he wanted to get down, and he continued to use foul language the whole time that he was lining them up against that wall," said Vargas.

BART surveillance footage showed Oscar walking off the train with Pirone next to him. Once Pirone had Oscar sitting against the wall with the others Karina Vargas turned her camera off, she said, because she thought it was just a routine stop. She soon realized how wrong she was and pressed the record button a second time.

" ... [B]ecause the noise started to pick up again, the cussing and the yelling, so that's when I stuck my head back out [of the train doors] and started recording again. Like I said, it was really just the aggressiveness that compelled me to tape record," Vargas said. Pirone had gone back to the train to retrieve Michael Greer – the other Black male with dark clothing he says he saw re-board the train - but the short trip to sit him against the station wall was far, far different from the way he escorted Oscar.

"Well, [Pirone] was like dragging the kid and with his, like all this body force, kind of like a walk/run, and then he just runs and slams him into the cement wall ... then he spun him around and threw him to the ground and he handcuffed him," remembers Pamela Caneva.

Keecha Williams, the train operator said she thought Pirone was engaged in a fight. " ... He was like jabbing; I see his arms, he was fighting somebody," she said. "When I see him, he's just punching towards someone in front of him." Her view was obstructed by a concrete wall, jutting out perpendicular to the back wall of the platform; thus she was unable to see and therefore, unaware of the fact that Pirone was the aggressor who had attacked Michael Greer.

Oscar, Reyes, and the Bryson brothers had been sitting as instructed by Pirone. Once Pirone attacked Greer, the young men leapt to their feet and verbally protested what was happening to their friend. Within a matter of seconds Pirone would unleash his wrath against Oscar Grant.

With slight variation, court witnesses Caneva, who was on the train looking out across at Oscar and his friends; Daniel Liu, who recorded what he saw from his location near the front (lead) car of the train; and Karina Vargas who was recording from the last car at the opposite end of the train, tell how Pirone's first assault of Oscar Grant unfolded:

"You fucking taking a picture of me?" Pirone yelled those words, according to Pamela Caneva, as he looked up from handcuffing Greer and saw Oscar, cell phone in hand, looking in Pirone's direction.

" ... and the officer gets up and he kind of hastily walks over to him screaming," continued Caneva, "... and he reaches where Oscar is sitting, and the next thing I know Oscar is standing against the wall ... I could only see the back of Officer Pirone and I could just see movement. I couldn't tell anything else."

Daniel Liu captured the scene by standing on top of his seat; moving from left to right, his video clearly shows Pirone getting up from kneeling over Greer and walking quickly over to the group just as Oscar Grant takes his hand and pats the chest of Jackie Bryson to his left. Pirone grabs and punches Oscar and then forces him and the others to sit against the wall, removing his Taser from his holster and pointing it at them. Liu said it looked like "rough shaking and punching" by Pirone. Karina Vargas' recollection is a bit more detailed. "I remember seeing the female officer there, and ... I'm pretty sure it was the male with the hat, he was saying something to the female officer and I saw Oscar put his hand on his friend's like chest like this ... that's when the male officer threw [Grant] up against the wall ... At that point ... Oscar then put his hands up like this and he slumped, like slid down to the wall onto his butt. He just slid down like that and had his hands raised," she said.

Karina Vargas' video, which moves from right to left, shows another angle of Pirone's first assault of Oscar that night, and the "male with the hat" that she referred to was Carlos Reyes who had been immediately to Oscar's right. Her recollection slightly conflicts with Vargas's testimony, but both Vargas' video and the one taken by Daniel Liu show Oscar raising his hand and patting the chest of Jackie Bryson, who was immediately to Oscar's left.

Vargas was clear that Oscar's gesture was a conciliatory one. When asked by Los Angeles Superior Court Judge Robert Perry if Grant's patting the chest of Jackie Bryson was "in the nature of a restraining ... or a calming down motion," Vargas replied in the affirmative. "From what it looked like to me, it seemed like his friend had maybe gotten a little bit smart with the female officer, and so what [Oscar] was trying to do was tell him like, 'Calm down; back up; don't get loud with her.' That's what it looked like to me," she said.

Her testimony underscores the accounts from Oscar's friends of his behavior on the platform that morning. They state that he attempted to keep his friends from lashing out at the BART officers, even though he himself was the object of verbal and physical attack. The time was now approximately 2:08 a.m. and the train had been sitting at the Fruitvale Station for just under 10 minutes. The BART passengers had already been restless; now they were angry. Audio from the recordings of the night clearly relays the passengers' verbal opinions of the police terror they are up close and personal witnesses to. When asked by the prosecutor, Alameda County Assistant District Attorney David Stein (ADA), if she had noticed a change in the noise level on the platform, Ms. Vargas said "It got louder.

Keecha Williams' view of the platform had been obscured but she saw enough to believe that Pirone was engaged in a fight. She put in a second call to BART dispatch and relayed that exact information.

Officer John Woffinden and his partner for the night, 27-year old Johannes Mehserle, had been at the West Oakland BART station prior to hearing the call of a fight on a train at the Fruitvale BART station. They arrived at Fruitvale as the call to assist a fellow officer came through. "At the time Officer Mehserle and I were standing at the bottom of the stairs and there was some sort of commotion up on the platform," said Woffinden. " … I wasn't sure [what was happening] … I just heard an officer hit an emergency button which indicated that he was requesting cover, and Officer Mehserle and I went - or started to go up the stairs to the platform," he said. BART Officers Emery Knudtson and Jonathan Guerra also headed to Fruitvale to provide assistance.

Once they arrived at Fruitvale's upstairs platform, Woffinden and Mehserle jogged toward where Domenici was keeping watch over Reyes, Oscar, and the Brysons. His Taser out, holding it in his right hand, Mehserle immediately proceeded to provide assistance to the BART officer. "Get back!" he yelled at some of the passengers who were now standing on the platform in close proximity to Domenici. "Get back!" he repeated as he moved closer to her, looking for direction. "Watch them," Domenici answered, referring to the four young men sitting in front of her.

Johntue Caldwell, Jamil Dewar Sophina Mesa and the others had been waiting for their friends to join them downstairs or let them know what was going on. Oscar and Sophina had known each other since their days at Mount Eden High School, eventually developing a romance that led to the birth of their daughter, Tatiana, in 2005. Sophina called Oscar on his cell phone as Caldwell and Dewar headed back upstairs to see what was keeping their friends.

"They're beating me up for no reason," Oscar said. Eyeing the young men sitting in front of him as well as scanning the surrounding crowd, Mehserle told Oscar to hang up his phone. "I gotta go," Oscar told Sophina as he sat against the wall. They would be his last words to her. Before hanging up with Sophina, Oscar took a picture of Johannes Mehserle standing in front of him with his Taser drawn seconds before Mehserle re-holstered it on the left side of his body.

"I'm gonna sue for police brutality!" Oscar stated. "Who … me?" Mehserle said he responded. He had still been trying to make heads or tails of the situation when Oscar made his claim.

"No not you, *him*," Oscar said, pointing at Pirone who was now walking towards them.

"Arrest those motherfuckers," Pirone snapped, pointing in Oscar and Jackie Bryson's direction. Pirone had been at the lead car talking with Keecha Williams, asking her if the young men who were seated against the wall were the ones who had been involved in the "fight" on the train. Williams hadn't seen the altercation so she could not identify anyone in the group and she told that to Pirone, yet Pirone made the decision to arrest the young men anyway.

Oscar rose to his feet, looking as if he was part inquiring-part protesting, "Who, me? What did I do?" Pirone's response was to press Oscar against the wall with his knee and forearm and force him back down to the ground. "Sit the fuck down!" he growled. Mehserle attempted to aid Pirone but now Jackie Bryson, immediately to Oscar's left also attempted to stand and protest what was occurring. By the time Pirone had given his order to arrest Oscar and Bryson, Mehserle had already re-holstered his Taser; after forcing Jackie Bryson back down to the platform floor, Mehserle took his Taser out again, holding it in his right hand and pointed it Bryson, telling him he didn't want any trouble out of him. Mehserle then put the Taser back into its holster on his left side and began to handcuff Bryson as Pirone stood in front of

Oscar.

A fifth officer, Jonathan Guerra, had now made his way onto the platform as passengers on the train once again loudly registered their disapproval of the BART officers' actions on that New Year's morning. Guerra stood closest to Mehserle and Pirone as Domenici and Woffinden created a barrier between the officers and the increasingly angry BART riders.

Oscar Grant was on parole from state prison at the time of this incident. Like all parolees, he would have to report any contact he had with police to his parole officer later on. It was possible that an arrest could return him to prison but it was not definite since, after all, it was New Year's Eve. Whether it was the thought of being removed from his family again or not being able to provide for his daughter Tatiana that was on Oscar's mind we will never know. What we do know is that Oscar is shown in the videos as being on his knees, facing Pirone in an obviously conciliatory position. According to Pirone's testimony, Oscar was telling him, "I have a four year-old daughter."

On the stand in Los Angeles Pirone testified that Grant's demeanor changed from one of concern to belligerence within a matter of seconds. According to Pirone, he thought Oscar's evoking of his daughter was "a way to get through to him," so he told Oscar, "What do you think your daughter would think about how you're acting right now?" At that exact moment, Pirone says, Oscar called him a "bitch ass nigger."

Neither Mehserle, nor Bryson nor Reyes - the three people closest to Oscar - testified that they heard Oscar utter those words to Pirone. Listening to the video, what Oscar says to Pirone is inaudible however, Pirone can be heard yelling those exact words at Oscar.

"There is an emotional as well as a physical component to any arrest," said Assistant District Attorney Stein to the court. "And when that emotional component is not held in check, bad things happen." Pirone's use of racial slurs toward Oscar Grant "stirred up" Johannes Mehserle and as a result, Stein argued, "… aggression takes over for training."

"Bitch ass nigger, huh? Bitch ass nigger, right? YEAH!"

Mehserle finished handcuffing Jackie Bryson and then moved to handcuff Oscar. Just as Pirone, standing in front of a kneeling Oscar Grant, repeated his words Mehserle can be seen attempting to slam Oscar down face first into the concrete deck of the Fruitvale BART Station.

Stein described the incident as a taunting and, he argued, Mehserle was working in tandem with his mentor and 'Big Brother" Tony Pirone, being given "the signal" to physically abuse Oscar by Pirone's racist taunting. Mehserle not only heard Pirone's words but, "… he reacted to them. He reacted to them by forcing Mr. Grant face down on the platform. He didn't need to do that," said Stein.

Karina Vargas' testimony echoed that assessment. "… I remember … they put Oscar on his belly to try to restrain him … [T]o me it looked like he had his hands behind his back voluntarily, like he didn't look like he was restraining, or resisting, excuse me," Vargas said.

"Bitch ass nigger, huh? Bitch ass nigger, right? YEAH!"

Pirone's words are defiantly and victoriously

stated, even hunching his shoulders for emphasis. The recordings by Daniel Liu and Tommy Cross, played in slow motion, showed Oscar Grant quickly bringing his right hand from behind his back and then placing it in front of him to break his fall. Mehserle's clumsy reaction to Oscar's movement turns Oscar Grant around almost 180 degrees to where Oscar is now on his back and briefly facing Mehserle.

The intention was to handcuff Oscar's hands behind him, not in front of him; but Mehserle has now fallen on top of Oscar and Pirone, in his rush to also inflict punishment on Oscar, immediately places the left knee of his 200-plus-pound frame on top of Oscar Grant's head even though Oscar is situated incorrectly. Mehserle, also weighing more than 200 pounds, fumbles to turn Oscar over while leaning onto Oscar's lower back and legs. Pirone has to begrudgingly give up his preferred position in order for Oscar to be placed onto his stomach.

Their actions could have been considered something out of a Three Stooges movie if the outcome had not been so deadly.

Oscar had been situated in between Jackie Bryson to his left and Carlos Reyes to his right. In all probability, since Mehserle was behind and slightly to the left of Oscar, he did not see that Reyes' left leg was outstretched so close to Oscar. But Oscar's right arm was now pinned beneath him, on top of Reyes' left leg, with more than 400-plus pounds of BART police pressing down on top of his 170-or-so-pound self on the concrete platform.

It must have felt like being trapped underneath a subway train.

"I can't breathe, I can't breathe. Just get off me,"

Oscar said.

As Oscar squirmed for relief, trying to get his breath, the only relief forthcoming would be by Pirone temporarily switching from his left knee to his right knee, using his hand to keep Oscar's head still.

"THAT'S FUCKED UP!" THAT'S FUCKED UP!"

Tommy Cross had been simply recording; now he was recording and yelling. Standing with other BART riders, he was looking out the train's open door directly across at what Pirone and Mehserle were doing to Oscar Grant. Unidentified BART riders all around Cross created a chorus of disapproval: "HEY!!" "HEY!!" "C'MON NOW! "REALLY?!"

"Give up your arms," Mehserle said he told Oscar. "I can't move, get off my neck," was Oscar's response. As Pirone switches from left knee to right knee Carlos Reyes, seated on the ground against the wall next to Oscar, begins to yell with his hands raised in the air, "He's on my leg! *He's on my leg!*" Reyes even attempts to point it out to the officers, hoping someone - anyone - will hear him. His cries fall on deaf ears.

The more Mehserle pulls at Oscar's right arm - pinned beneath Oscar and on top of Reyes' leg - the more it is not forthcoming. According to Mehserle who is oblivious to both this fact *and* the location of Pirone, who is on top of Oscar Grant's head, Oscar Grant is reaching into his front pants pocket for a gun.

Mehserle and Woffinden had responded to a call earlier in the evening of a man with a gun at the West Oakland train station. The individual, who was eventually apprehended by BART officers, had jumped from the elevated platform to the ground below and tried to run. Once he was caught police "said" they found a small firearm in his front right pants pocket. The adrenalin of pursuing a fleeing suspect who would be found with a gun on his person probably had not completely subsided yet; and then Mehserle and Woffinden heard the call that a fellow BART officer needed assistance at Fruitvale Station, so they hurriedly made their way there.

"I'm going to tase him."

Mehserle said he told Pirone that he was going to tase Oscar Grant, ostensibly because he could not get Oscar's right arm out from beneath him. In court Pirone testified that Mehserle told him to get back. Jackie Bryson, with hands cuffed behind his back, was kneeling next to Oscar, Pirone and Mehserle while all of this was happening. He too, testified in court that he heard Mehserle say "I'm going Tase him." But Jackie Bryson also testified that he heard Mehserle say something else: "Fuck this."

The video footage clearly showed Johannes Mehserle using his right hand and tugging at his black .40 caliber Sig Sauer automatic handgun weighing about a pound and a half, located on the right side of his holster. His Taser International X-26 taser, a bright yellow-colored weapon weighing about a pound, was located on the left side of his holster. Mehserle had held and re-holstered the taser with his right hand twice that night; even being captured in a photo by Oscar Grant with the weapon pointed directly at Oscar's chest.

"Fuck this."

Mehserle is tugging at his service revolver while still kneeling, even glancing at it once. As he works at unhooking the weapon from his holster, he slowly begins to rise up off of a prone Oscar Grant. As his weight lifts, Carlos Reyes is able to slide his left leg out from beneath Oscar Grant, and Oscar is able to bring his right arm from underneath his body and place it on his back, palm up, but it is too late. Johannes Mehserle is now standing up behind Oscar, looking downward with both hands on his service weapon. He fires one shot directly into Oscar's back, barely giving Tony Pirone any time to move out of the way.

It would be the "shot heard round the world," as they say, thanks to the wonder of YouTube.

Expressions of shock and horror reverberate throughout the Fruitvale Station platform. The entire train station lets out a collective gasp of "OHHHH!" once the shot is fired. The shock of the moment appears to last for a few seconds. Carlos Reyes, to the right of Oscar sitting with both hands raised, jumps slightly and grabs at his baseball cap as he looks at his friend who has just been shot in the back; Jackie Bryson, on his knees to the left of Oscar Grant, immediately jumps to his feet, speechless, looking from Oscar to Mehserle and Pirone, and then back down at Oscar lying on the ground; Mehserle looks at Oscar, then Pirone with a perplexed look on his face and then back down at Oscar Grant; Pirone's facial expression cannot be seen. From the back, he appears to look down at Oscar Grant and then at Mehserle.

The shock of what has just occurred begins to wear off as the ugly reality registers on all those who are present.

"Oh shit! He just shot that guy!" said Daniel Liu, located near the lead car, recording the incident standing on top of a seat.

"What the fuck?! FUCK!" yelled Tommy Cross, recording directly across from Oscar Grant.

"They just shot him! … They just shot him! … I got you muthafuckas" shouted Karina Vargas. Vargas had been moving back and forth between the platform and the far end of the train, her device recording the entire time. She turned her camera briefly to catch Officer Emery Knudtsen handcuffing Fernando Anicette on the ground when the gunshot can be clearly heard. She quickly turned back toward the area where Oscar Grant was being held. Her camera captures Oscar's head for what seems like a nanosecond and then turns to the floor, as if Vargas had removed the camera from in front of her face to make sure she was seeing what she thought she was seeing.

Vargas explained that she said "I got you "muthafuckas" because she knew she had video evidence of a crime being committed by law enforcement.

Jackie Bryson begins screaming at Mehserle and Pirone, standing and trying to straddle Oscar's mortally wounded body; a valiant attempt to protect his friend even though Bryson is still handcuffed. Mehserle goes from having a perplexed look on his face, to placing both hands on his head quickly, to attempting to calm both Bryson and Oscar down.

Other BART train riders are cursing, yelling, screaming. Johntue Caldwell, who had been kept at bay from his friends by the other BART officers, angrily throws his cell phone in their direction, shattering it to pieces. He missed, but the point was made. Fernando Anicette, who Karina Vargas had videotaped being handcuffed by Knudtsen, had actually been tackled to the ground by the officer, adding to the anger of the train riders. Jamil Dewar, filming the chaos from the far end of the platform on his cell phone as he walked toward his friends, heard the shot but did not see it. Something or someone told him it was Oscar who had been shot because he began to ask, he began to yell, *"They shot my cousin? They shot my cousin?"* An affirmative answer to Dewar's pleading cannot be heard but within seconds, Dewar no longer asks but declares "THEY SHOT MY COUSIN!"

At the trial in Los Angeles, the 17-year old Dewar broke down crying uncontrollably on the witness stand during the replay of his video. Judge Perry ordered a short recess and cleared the court but not before the jury saw Dewar's mother, also sobbing loudly, run from the spectator bench in the back of the room to hold and comfort her child.

"YOU SHOT ME! I HAVE A 4-YEAR OLD DAUGHTER!" said Oscar Grant.

Turning over onto his side, Oscar moved as if to get up from the pavement. "Why'd you shoot me?!" He asked. Mehserle knelt down and placed his hands on Oscar to keep him from getting up.

"'Calm down, calm down,' I told him, Mehserle testified. "You're going to be alright."

But Oscar wasn't going to be alright. The bullet from Mehserle's .40 caliber Sig Sauer had entered the left side of Oscar's body through his lower back, traveling diagonally through several organs and his right lung, exiting and ricocheting off the concrete platform beneath, and then back into his chest. He was transported to Oakland's Highland Hospital but his right lung had collapsed and doctors were unable to stop him from bleeding internally. Oscar Juliuss Grant, III, was pronounced dead a little after 9 a.m., on January 1, 2009. He was 22 years old.

"AW HELL NAW!"

The voice is undoubtedly that of a Black woman captured on Tommy Cross' video. To this day her identity is unknown, but her words spoke as much to the disbelief of what had just been witnessed on the Fruitvale BART platform as it did to the attitude that would be adopted by an angry city in the days to come: the attitude of 'this will not stand.'

The doors to the BART train close and Tommy Cross' video cuts off just after the woman's words ring out.

"AW HELL NAW!"

CHAPTER TWO

Lies and Damn Lies

Johannes Mehserle's claim that he meant to pull his taser on Oscar Grant but accidentally grabbed his gun instead was a damn lie, and his defense team's determination to force this lie down the public's throat was arrogant, vile and vulgar. In addition to insisting that we believe this damn lie, the amount of *anger* from Mehserle supporters at calls for accountability in the murder of a young Black man by a white police officer revealed classic white supremacist characteristics of remorselessness, disdain and ambivalence toward the violent, racist and unjust acts inflicted against Black people.

Paul Kivel is a nationally known activist, author and trainer who has noted the similarities between the widespread excuses that are used for white supremacy and the excuses of men who are abusive to women and children. Kristian Williams, author of *Our Enemies in Blue: Police and Power in America*, takes note of Kivel's work and shows how these same excuses are analogous to police terrorism:

Minimization:

Domestic Abuser	"It was only a slap"
Police	"Police use force infrequently"
Mehserle's Defense	"It was an accident"

Redefinition:

Domestic Abuser	"It was mutual combat"
Police	"The subject was resisting arrest"
Mehserle's Defense	Oscar Grant was resisting arrest"

Unintentionality:

Domestic Abuser	"Things got out of hand"
Police	"Officers had no choice but to use deadly force"
Mehserle's Defense	"I meant to tase him"

Such excuses are the lies that comprise the "bag of tricks" that all abusers – be they violent husbands and boyfriends or sworn representatives of the state – use in their attempts to escape responsibility for their actions. The second murder of Oscar Grant begins with the damn lies, at least seven of them, that were stated about him in various legal documents that were filed before Mehserle's trial actually begin in Los Angeles in 2010 and uttered later on once the trial began. The legal documents, taken at face value as truthful and correct, would lay the basis for the media's third murder of Oscar Grant.

The only purpose of these lies was to minimize Johannes Mehserle's responsibility for the physical murder of Oscar Grant. The remainder of this chapter analyzes six of these lies in detail.

1. Oscar Grant was fighting with someone on the train

Although BART train operator Keecha Williams was not able to see who was involved in the altercation on her train as it pulled into the Fruitvale station, she did not state that the crowd was behaving in a manner that would suggest people were trying to get out of the way of a melee, a free-for-all. In her testimony in Los Angeles, Williams effortlessly described the altercation as "nothing."

David Horowitch, the man identified as actually being in the "altercation," testified during a preliminary hearing in Oakland that, "I didn't get in no fight that night," and, "I have no problem with Oscar Grant." Michael Rains, Mehserle's defense attorney accused Horowitch of downplaying the incident since, in Rains' words, Horowitch was a former felon on parole and admitting to being in a fight would cause his parole to be revoked. During the preliminary hearing in Oakland, CA in 2009, Rains asked Horowitch if he was afraid that testifying would bring repercussions to him or his family; Horowitch answered, "I feel more fear from police than anyone because I'm being harassed."

Since this would have clashed with Mehserle's narrative, Rains did not call Horowitch to testify during the criminal trial in Los Angeles. Rains opted instead to show the jurors Horowitch's picture. From the photograph Horowitch's ethnicity appears to be Caucasian however it is not exactly known; upon first sight one would think he is a white man. This may have been the impression Rains had hoped for – a white man accosted and assaulted by uncontrollable

Black youth – when he continually flashed Horowitch's photo to the jurors in the Los Angeles trial.

Michael Rains, by the way, is a former United States Marine who served in Vietnam. After leaving the Marine Corps Rains became a police officer in Santa Monica, CA. It was during his stint as a police officer that he was awarded a scholarship to attend law school. Michael Rains is currently one of the top "go to" attorneys in the state of California for police officers accused of misconduct. Prior to defending Johannes Mehserle Rains was the attorney who defended the "Corcoran 8," prison guards accused of setting up "gladiator fights" between inmates in Corcoran Prison, and the "Oakland Riders," four members of the Oakland, CA police department accused by 119 people of some form of misconduct – kidnappings, planting evidence, and beatings. Rains won acquittals in both cases.

Carlos Reyes, one of Oscar Grant's friends, was called next by Rains to testify about the altercation that had occurred on the train. Reyes was a part of the group that went to the Embarcadero and returned on BART; he was detained with Oscar Grant on the Fruitvale platform; Reyes was closest to Grant when Mehserle shot him; and Reyes was held handcuffed for six hours afterwards in a BART police station, and eventually released with no charges. Rains attempted to intimidate and grill Reyes into saying that a fight had occurred between Grant and Horowitch. Reyes consistently described the altercation as a non-altercation: he stated that the train was so crowded that no blows could have been thrown had participants wanted to, and he called the altercation a "scuffle," in spite of Rains' insistence otherwise.

Jackie Bryson, another one of Oscar's friends detained that night and also called by Rains, testified that there was a "struggle," not a fight, and he said "It was more wrestling, but they could have punched each other. It was more like a wrestling match."

Husband-and-wife Dennis and Agnes Zafiratos were the ones who placed the initial call to train operator Williams of a fight on a train. Dennis testified he told the train operator "it was Black males" involved in the disturbance, conveniently leaving out both Horowitch's presence and his actions. On the other hand, Agnes' testimony on the witness stand was very specific in regards to Horowitch; she said he stood out to her, "… because he was fair, number one; he had on a big white t-shirt, an oversized t-shirt, a lighter pair of jeans and a white pair of like shoes, tennis shoes, so he just stood out in the crowd ... he was the one that was punching – he was the one that had the person in a headlock," she said, and "was punching him … body punches … at least five or six." Although both Reyes and Bryson testified they did not see how the altercation started, both said the person Horowitch had in the headlock was Oscar Grant.

Based on this testimony of all four individuals, it appears that tempers flared on the train and that a pushing and shoving match ensued; and, had there been enough room for punches to be have been thrown freely, it more than likely would have happened; and yet, the main punches that occurred appeared to have been made by Horowitch at Oscar Grant's body while in a headlock. Dennis Zafiratos described arms flailing in what looked to be an overhand, overhead punch, but this was attributed to Jackie Bryson, not Oscar Grant.

A great deal was made about this "fight" by Rains. In spite of the inconsistencies, denials and minimizations in the testimony, the issue of self-defense was never raised – not even by the prosecutor who is supposed to represent the people in a criminal matter (which people?) The idea that Oscar Grant could have been defending himself from someone who may have been the aggressor (Horowitch) was not raised during this trial; no room was made to give Oscar Grant the benefit of the doubt, that perhaps he had been assaulted. Oscar Grant was simply assumed to have been the aggressor because he *may* have been *involved* in a fight, which translates implicitly to being an equal participant in a fight. Oscar Grant was resoundingly condemned by both inference through Mehserle's defense and by supporters of law enforcement throughout coverage of the case as having caused his own death: "if he hadn't been fighting or causing trouble on the train, he would still be alive" were and continue to be the most common comments regarding who is culpable in Oscar Grant's death.

Although Horowitch appears physically to be a white man, and at least two of Oscar Grant's friends (including his fiance') are Latino, the charge made by Dennis Zafiratos and relayed to BART police was that a "large group of Black males, black clothing" were involved in a fight. Dennis Zafiratos' white supremacist clouded observation, which zeroed in on only the "black males" led to the "racial profiling" employed by Tony Pirone as he made his way onto the Fruitvale platform.

NO DOUBT: THE MURDER(S) OF OSCAR GRANT

2. Oscar Grant was high on drugs and drunk

The origin of the damn lie that Oscar was high *and* drunk rests in Michael Rains' motion for bail that will be discussed in detail in Chapter Three. Still, this testimony from Johannes Mehserle bears witnessing:

Stein: Did you have any basis to believe that Mr. Grant was under the influence of any drugs, much less P.C.P.?

Mehserle: No, sir, I didn't ... there was no indication that he didn't appear to be under any drugs, sir.

3. Oscar Grant attempted to assault Officer Pirone by kneeing him in the groin

The purpose of this damn lie was to paint Oscar Grant as a violent thug who had no qualms about assaulting a police officer, thus justifying the "use of force" against him in the last few seconds of his life. This lie was uttered in court by Mehserle's attorney Michael Rains and his expert video witness Michael Schott. And yet it was BART officer Tony Pirone who physically assaulted Oscar Grant three times on the morning of Jan. 1, 2009 within a span of 10 minutes. The first assault occurred after Grant and his friends reacted to Pirone's vicious assault of Michael Greer.

In his testimony during both the preliminary hearing in the summer of 2009 in Alameda Superior Court and during the trial in Los Angeles, Pirone stated that Michael Greer pushed himself into the wall on the platform, bounced off and turned around with fists clenched as if he was going to throw a punch at Pirone. "Fists clenched" is key language that an officer must use when getting his story straight; it's considered to be a "signal" to the officer that a person is about to or may act aggressively toward him, which is why Pirone chose that language in spite of eyewitness testimony that no such action occurred. Pirone then said he used the "sweep" technique to knock Greer off of his feet, where he then turned him on his stomach and handcuffed him.

Grant, Reyes and the Brysons had been sitting against the wall as Pirone retrieved Greer from the train. Once Pirone began his attack of Greer, the four young men stood up and verbally protested Pirone's actions. In the video we are able to see Pirone walking toward the young men, grabbing Grant and assaulting him in the upper body area before eventually pushing Grant to a sitting position on the ground. It is while Pirone is grabbing Grant, just prior to forcing him to sit down, that Rains and Schott, a forensic video image analyst, claim that Oscar Grant attempted to knee Pirone in the groin. Pirone, under oath, stated on the witness stand that he did not remember Oscar Grant attempting to assault him.

Pirone said his actions toward Michael Greer were predicated on the belief that Greer was about to physically assault him and so he "took him down." The physical space between Pirone and Greer was greater than the space between himself and Grant however, Pirone's response to such an obvious, aggressive and potentially painful possible assault on his person as being kneed in the groin was to simply sit Oscar Grant down and then walk away from him? His response was to go back to the train to speak with operator Keecha Williams? Although Grant was attacked by Pirone he was not viciously subdued – something one would reasonably expect after a "suspect" has just tried to assault a police officer by kneeing him in the groin. Grant was not immediately restrained with handcuffs like Greer was, nor was he immediately placed under arrest. He was simply left 'guarded' by Pirone's partner Marisol Domenici. We are therefore asked to believe that this was both a consistent and credible response by a law enforcement officer – a former Marine no less – to such a potentially violent – and painful – assault against his person; it was neither.

4.   Oscar Grant called Pirone a 'bitch ass nigger'

It is quite possible, even probable that *someone* yelled the words 'bitch ass nigger' at Anthony Pirone on that New Year's morning; a BART train rider, maybe even one of Oscar's friends, but to request that we accept the scenario that Pirone described in his testimony – that those words came from Oscar Grant as he was on his knees pleading with the 200-plus pound, former Marine who had already attacked him *and* had threatened to tase him – is a bit much at the least and insulting at the worst.

Tommy Cross' video of Jan. 1, 2009, provides both the clearest video and audio of Tony Pirone calling Oscar Grant a 'bitch ass nigger.' Pirone can be seen standing directly in front of Oscar with his back to the camera; Oscar Grant is on his knees facing Pirone; Pirone can be seen leaning forward slightly and hunching his shoulders, as he is yelling the racial slur at Oscar. Both Pirone and Mehserle's defense team stated that Pirone was not taunting Grant, but simply responding to what Oscar Grant had said to Pirone – Pirone claimed that Oscar called him that name first.

By the time Johannes Mehserle fatally shot Oscar Grant a few seconds after Pirone utters those words, the Fruitvale train platform was an incredibly noisy area. BART train riders had been consistently registering their disapproval of BART police actions; Jackie Bryson testified that his younger brother Nigel was also yelling at the police. In terms of what Oscar Grant may have said to Pirone when the officer first removed him from the train, there is no record and we may never truly know.

Pirone testified that at approximately 2:08 a.m. - mere seconds before Johannes Mehserle shoots Grant in the back - he asked Oscar what would his daughter think about how he was acting? What Pirone is referring to when he speaks about "how Oscar Grant was acting" is a mystery from observing the videos *and* Pirone's own testimony. Pirone actually testified that Oscar Grant told him he respected the police: "… I remember him saying something along the lines of 'why are you messing with me, I respect the police, I got a four-year-old daughter." Prosecutor Stein then attempted to make sense of Pirone's statement:

Stein: Other than him saying at that point that he had a four-year-old daughter, do you [recall] him saying anything else?

Pirone: Well, at that point, I was like, I think I even asked him, well if you got a kid, what would she think if she saw you acting like this, and that's when he called me, pardon my language, but 'a bitch ass nigga.' He says 'you're a bitch ass nigga.'

Stein: So if I understand this correctly, Mr. Grant goes from telling you that he has a four-year-old daughter in one moment to the following moment when he's calling you 'a bitch ass nigga.' Is that what your testimony is?

Pirone: Yeah, after I asked him about what his daughter would think if she saw him acting this way towards police, because he just got through telling me he respects police, but here he is saying those words.

From a purely common sense standpoint, such a scenario is neither consistent nor credible for us to believe that Oscar Grant 1) spoke "belligerently" or "defiantly" to a police officer who has already assaulted him twice within a span of ten minutes while he was on his knees in front of said officer, or 2) that he switched gears from speaking in a beseeching and submissive demeanor to one of belligerence and defiance in the span of two-to-three seconds.

Besides, such a response as the one alleged by Pirone would more than likely have been prefaced with the words "fuck you" and then followed by other profanities if it had actually occurred.

5. Oscar Grant resisted arrest on Oct. 15, 2006 and he had to be tased; he was therefore "prone" to resisting

Part of Michael Rains' defense strategy for his client was to establish that Oscar Grant was resisting arrest when Johannes Mehserle decided to tase him. To do this Rains sought to characterize Oscar as a person who was "prone" to resisting arrest. Rains asked for and received permission to submit as evidence a police report from the San Leandro Police Department of Oscar Grant's arrest on Oct. 15, 2006 and he called the arresting officer and author of the report, 8-year veteran Alex Hidas, to testify in Los Angeles.

Basically, Rains' line of reasoning consisted of "Oscar Grant had to be tased before, and he had to be tased this time, too." Judge Robert Perry gave the jurors a "limiting instruction" prior to Hidas' testimony wherein he stated:

> ... from time to time, a court will give what is called a 'limiting instruction' regarding evidence and how you may consider evidence. And in this case, one of the issues in this trial is whether Oscar Grant resisted BART officers' commands on Jan. 1st, 2009. ... You're going to be hearing about an incident that occurred ... involving San Leandro Sheriff's Deputies, and you may consider this evidence only as it may relate to Oscar Grant's possible resistance on Jan. 1st of 2009, and for no other purpose.

Unlike Oscar's murder, there is no filmed record of his 2006 arrest by Hidas, therefore, we will never know the truth of what really occurred on the evening of Oct. 15th in San Leandro, the neighboring city immediately south of Oakland.

According to Hidas' report, he was working alone that night patrolling the south end of the city around 9:15 p.m. when he noticed a car driving towards him with its high beam lights on. Hidas says he was temporarily blinded for a moment, and after the car passed him he turned his vehicle around and began a pursuit to initiate a traffic stop.

The following excerpt is from Hidas' testimony at the criminal trial in Los Angeles and will be quoted extensively:

> I noticed that there were three occupants in the vehicle. Since I was working alone, it was nighttime, I requested a backup unit, backup unit was dispatched to assist me, I made contact with the driver, with the front passenger and eventually Mr. Grant, who was sitting in the backseat. I noticed that he was not wearing a seat belt, so I requested that he produce identification. As Mr. Grant began to check his pockets for identification I noticed that he brushed the left side of his jacket away from his body and placed his left hand on his left front pant pocket. At that time, I observed an item of contraband in his left front pant pocket. I immediately told Mr. Grant to place both of his hands on the headrest in front of him, I told the driver to place both hands on the steering wheel, I told the front seat passenger to lean forward and place both

hands on the dashboard, I told all three men not to move, and I drew my firearm for my own safety and waited for backup. … the driver and the front seat passenger continued to comply, meaning they did not move from where I instructed them to not move from. However, Mr. Grant removed – took his right hand off of the headrest and began to bring it down to his side out of my view. I pointed my firearm at Mr. Grant, and I ordered him to place his hand back on the headrest and not to move … I was standing on the driver's side of the vehicle at the rear passenger's seat area - excuse me, rear door, just outside of the rear door. The muzzle of my gun was probably about three to four feet maybe away from him.

Hidas went on to testify that he repeated his command and that although Oscar Grant made eye contact with him, "he did not listen to my command. He opened the passenger door, exited the vehicle and begin [sic] to run away through the parking lot."

As a quick recap: we are first asked to view this as credible and true: that Oscar Grant was able to open a car door and run from a police officer who has drawn a gun on him from a distance of "three to four feet" and told him not to move; we are asked to believe that this officer who drew his gun and gave this command did not then open fire on Oscar, even though he stated that he "noticed" Oscar was armed.

Hidas continued, saying that he chased after Grant on foot and yelled for Grant to stop and get on the ground but that Grant kept on running. Hidas was then joined in the chase by Officer Warren deGuzman who responded to his call for backup. After trying to cut Grant off with his vehicle, Hidas stated deGuzman exited the vehicle and also gave chase wherein he was in closer proximity to Grant. Hidas estimated that he was perhaps 100 to 150 away from Grant and that once deGuzman began to catch up with Grant, deGuzman drew his taser and pointed it at Grant. Hidas then testified that:

> I saw him [deGuzman] fire his taser at Mr. Grant, and the taser appeared to strike Mr. Grant in the back, because his body positioning began to change, he started to fall down, he started to stumble, begin to flail his arms, and it looked like he was starting to go to the ground ... *Mr. Grant had thrown the item of contraband and it landed in the parking lot of a gas station that they were running toward at that time.* Mr. Grant ended up falling head first into a parked vehicle that was parked on the parking lot of the gas station, and he fell in front of that vehicle, and officer deGuzman was about - he had caught up to him by then. [Emphasis mine].

Hidas says that it appeared to him that Oscar Grant struck his head on the front end of a car, "... closer to the front tire of the engine compartment ...", and that once he caught up to where Grant and deGuzman were, he was on the left side of Oscar Grant and deGuzman was on the right side, and that Hidas "... saw that the upper portion of Mr. Grant's body was underneath the front end of that car, and his left hand was no longer visible ..." At this point, deGuzman begins ordering Oscar Grant to show him his hands but Grant is not responding, which is not surprising since Oscar had just been shocked with a taser *and* had fallen head first into a car. In his police report Hidas says:

> Officer deGuzman and I both ordered Grant to show us his hands, but he did not bring his left arm or hand behind his back or into our view. *Since, I believed Grant was armed and had a weapon in his left front pant pocket*, and he refused to show me his left hand, I kicked Grant in the left side of his upper body (about 2-3 times) until he brought his hand behind his back. Grant was detained in hand cuffs without further incident. [Emphasis mine].

To justify kicking Grant "2-3 times," Hidas blatantly contradicts himself in his police report writing in one instance that he sees Oscar Grant throw the gun – the one Hidas determined was in Oscar's left front pants pocket - in his possession into the air, and in the next instance Hidas writes that he believes Grant is armed with a weapon in his left font pants pocket.

Additionally, Hidas' language characterizes this incident as Oscar Grant intentionally keeping his hand from him, stating in his testimony in Los Angeles that Grant continued to keep his left hand underneath for "about five to ten seconds." In his police report Hidas says that he was concerned both for his own safety and that of deGuzman, and thus continued to keep his gun pointed at Grant because he believed him to be armed. Hidas later notes in his report that, "Officer deGuzman advised me that Grant vomited and was injured during his arrest. Grant complained of pain in his back, the left side of his head, and his left knee. He had an abrasion on his left knee and was limping." Hidas ends the report by saying Oscar Grant was transported to San Leandro Hospital for his injuries.

Officer deGuzman, who did not testify in the Los Angeles trial, wrote the following account about his tasering of Oscar Grant in his police report:

> I continued to run southbound after Grant from his blind side, on his right, across Lewelling Bl. As I got within the taser's 21-ft shooting range, I pointed the red laser dot at Grant's rear center body mass and pulled the trigger. I saw a prong enter Grant's jacket and knew I had hit my mark. Grant then began to stumble forward as his momentum carried. I continued to run forward as well in order to keep the prong intact. Grant finally collapsed to the ground where he hit his head on the side of a parked

... When Grant collided with the parked vehicle, I saw a small black object fly into the air over the parked vehicle. When Grant tried crawling underneath the parked vehicle where I could not see his hands, I continued to depress the taser trigger. After Grant continued to resist, I executed a right foot strike to the right side of Grant's ribs and ordered Grant to show me his hands. Grant finally cooperated and placed his right hand to his side.

deGuzman also uses language in his report that characterizes Oscar Grant as intentionally keeping his hands underneath him, resisting and trying to crawl underneath the parked car that he has just hit his head on. Steve Tuttle, spokesman of Taser International, the Scottsdale, Arizona company that manufactures the Taser X26 that deGuzman deployed on Oscar Grant, says that their 50,000 volt product is "designed to cause neuro-muscular incapacitation," and affect a person's "ability to do any coordinated action" for five seconds.

deGuzman says he depressed the trigger on his taser a second time when Oscar Grant did not immediately produce his hands. Let us look carefully at what we have here: the temporary inability of a person to immediately produce his or her hands, place them on their back and/or follow any other commands directed by police after sustaining two electric shocks to the body – which causes a locking up of the muscles and involuntary actions of the body – as well as hitting their head on a parked car and possibly suffering a mild concussion and/or blacking out. In spite of the above, we are asked to believe that Oscar Grant was in control of his faculties enough to willfully resist arrest and thus it was a natural inclination, according to Michael Rains – something Oscar was "prone" to do.

It most assuredly was not.

6. Oscar Grant was resisting arrest on Jan. 1, 2009

Any lack of response or hesitancy to quickly follow a police officer's commands, as well as any type of voluntary or involuntary movement, is usually considered 'resisting arrest.' More sinister, however, is the fact that the concept of "resisting arrest" is a catch-all phrase that effectively and completely ab – solves all police from any accountability, culpability, responsibility, criminality *whatsoever* when they commit the crime of murdering Black people in particular.

This particular damn lie about Oscar Grant resisting arrest is somewhat convoluted and will take some time to unravel fully.

At the time of his murder on Jan. 1, 2009, Oscar was on parole from state prison. Michael Rains' defense argument was that since Grant was on parole and his contact with BART police could have sent him back to state prison, he resisted in order to keep from being arrested.

According to Rains' story, Tony Pirone makes the decision to arrest Oscar "for 148", which is the section of California's Penal Code that talks about people who either resist arrest or obstruct an officer in his or her investigation. To bolster its claim the defense called Greg Meyer, a retired Los Angeles Police Department (LAPD) captain and use of force expert, who stated that Oscar Grant's re-boarding of the train at Fruitvale was an effort to evade Pirone and could be considered resisting arrest or obstructing an officer from the performance of his duties.

Meyer continued by claiming that Oscar Grant's (and by extension Jackie and Nigel Bryson also) standing up when told to sit down against the wall was also an act of resisting arrest. Continuing with the "resisting arrest" theme, Pirone had stated that, once he placed his knee (that was connected to his 200-plus pound frame) on Oscar Grant's head, Oscar was attempting to "wiggle away" from him. Meyer supported Pirone's claim by characterizing those particular actions of Oscar Grant's as "Evasive movements, twisting, turning."

No one testified that they believed Oscar Grant's movements while pinned underneath the combined 400-plus pounds of Pirone and Mehserle were from extreme pain or an assertion of his human rights.

This would be a good point at which to pause and mention exactly who Greg Meyer is: a 30-year veteran of the LAPD, Meyer was also an expert witness during the "Rodney King Trial." He was called by the defense during the civil trial and was a consultant for the defense during the sentencing phase of the criminal trial of the four police officers who attempted to murder King in 1991. Meyer has bemoaned the LAPD's loss of the "choke hold," also known as the carotid neck restraint. The "choke hold" had been used by police to murder Black and Brown men in Los Angeles for decades. Meyer wrote that the use of batons was a direct result of officers no longer being able to use the "choke hold."

The "jumping – back – onto – the – train – as – a – form – of – resisting – arrest" story is part one of a two-part lie that defense attorney Michael Rains promoted in court. The second part however, the one he hammered home, was that as Mehserle tried to handcuff Oscar Grant, Oscar was "putting himself on the ground, throwing his shoulder down and rolling on his back" and that he was "… going forward and actively resisting." This happens after Pirone has given the order for the arrest to be made.

Anthony Pirone comes back to the area of the platform where Grant, Reyes and the Brysons are after speaking with the train operator Keecha Williams. He points at Grant saying that he's under arrest when Oscar Grant begins to stand up from where he has been sitting against the wall. At that point, defense attorney Rains says, both Mehserle and Pirone push Grant back down to the ground and Pirone "… moves in and appears to place a knee against Mr. Grant who is now against the wall having been pushed down to the ground by Officer Mehserle." Jackie Bryson also tries to stand up and is restrained by Mehserle. Mehserle is then joined by another BART officer, Jonathan Guerra, and they both put handcuffs on Jackie Bryson. According to Rains rambling defense narrative the rest of the story goes like this:

> " … Mr. Mehserle turns his attention to Oscar Grant. Oscar Grant is under arrest. Oscar Grant is against the wall. He appears to be seated and Mr. Mehserle moves in behind Oscar Grant to handcuff him … and he

grabs at Mr. Grant's hand ... and he gets Mr. Grant up to his knees. And then when Mr. Grant is up to his knees, all of a sudden he starts moving forward. And so Grant starts going to the ground ... Grant starts moving forward from the wall, and as he moves forward from the wall his right hand comes out from behind him, and as he comes out from behind him his shoulder goes down to the ground and he rolls onto his back ... And for the next 12 seconds Mehserle is now holding onto Grant's hands and grappling with him and trying to get control of those hands and it's not happening. And at 2:10:49 [a.m.], finally Pirone is able to get a hold of Mr. Grant's shoulder and turns him over ... Officer Mehserle gets over to Mr. Grant's right side and Mr. Grant's hands are now underneath him. They're down by his stomach. He's on his stomach and Mehserle and Pirone are yelling, "Give us your hands, give us your hands." And Mr. Grant's hands stay under him. And Mehserle and Pirone are both demanding that he give up his hands, and Mehserle is using his force to tug on Mr. Grant's right arm. The hand isn't coming out. The hand isn't coming out, and this is witnessed by a number of people ...".

Slow motion analysis of the videos by Daniel Liu, taken at the head of the BART train and by Tommy Cross in the middle of the train almost directly across from Pirone, Grant and Mehserle, clearly show this damn lie for what it is: Oscar Grant with his right hand voluntarily going behind his back, obeying the officers' commands while still attempting to plead with Pirone; Johannes Mehserle attempting to slam Oscar face first into the concrete pavement of the Fruitvale platform in response to Tony Pirone's racial slur directed at Oscar Grant; Oscar Grant quickly pulling his right hand from behind his back and placing it in front of him in an attempt to protect himself from being slammed into the pavement by Johannes Mehserle; Mehserle reacting and falling on top of Oscar Grant, turning Oscar over; Pirone then placing his knee on Oscar Grant's head and neck, switching from left knee to right knee at some point; Johannes Mehserle attempting to remove his black .40 Sig Sauer service weapon from its holster on the right side of his body for several seconds, even looking directly at the gun on at least one occasion; Carlos Reyes, sitting against the wall next to Oscar Grant with his hands raised yelling, "He's on my leg!" in the hopes that the two officers will realize the chaos they have caused; Mehserle rising to shoot Oscar Grant in the back; Carlos Reyes pulling his left leg from under Oscar Grant and moving it out of the way; Oscar Grant finally being able to pull his right arm out from underneath him and place it on his back now that Mehserle has gotten off of him; Johannes Mehserle holding his service weapon with both hands, aiming into Oscar Grant's back and pulling the trigger.

Oscar Grant had placed his hands behind his back in compliance with BART police officer Anthony Pirone's initial orders. Johannes Mehserle's attempt to slam Oscar Grant face first into the pavement, acting in tandem with Pirone to use the words of the prosecutor, is what created both the situation that pinned Oscar's right arm underneath him and the struggle to get Oscar to "give up" his right arm. Had Johannes Mehserle *not* undertaken this specific action Oscar Grant would have left the Fruitvale BART station alive on Jan. 1, 2009. Mehserle was easily able to handcuff Oscar without the need to slam him into the pavement; his own testimony admits that Oscar's hands were initially behind his back:

Stein: Now, I'm stopping [the video] at frame number 2049. Do you see Mr. Grant's hands in front of him in this image?

Mehserle: Yes, sir.

Stein: And now we're going to go frame by frame forward and I'd like to see if you can tell me what he does with his hands.

Mehserle: Okay. His -- it appears that now he put his hands behind his back, yes, sir.

Stein: He did that voluntarily, didn't he?

Mehserle: I believe -- I don't know. I'm not -- it looks like it, yes, sir.

Stein: Well, do you remember having to phy-

	sically force him to put his hands behind his back?
Mehserle:	No, I remember his hands being behind his back. I thought it was going to be as routine as Mr. Bryson, sir.
Stein:	Did you have to apply any control holds to Mr. Grant in order to get him to put his hands behind his back?
Mehserle:	No, sir.
Stein:	Did Officer Pirone ever have to put any control holds on Mr. Grant to get him to put his hands behind his back?
Mehserle:	Not that I know of.
Stein:	As you sit there now, can you think of any conduct or action of Mr. Grant that suggested he did anything other than voluntarily put his hands behind his back?
Judge Perry:	At this point?
Stein:	At this point?
Mehserle:	At this point, no, sir.

Despite this, Michael Rains continued his libeling and slurring of Oscar Grant saying that Oscar was "... trying to get out, away from officer Pirone and undoubtedly Mr. Mehserle as well," because he was not laying motionless under the combined 400-plus-pounds of the two BART officers and that, at the time of Johannes Mehserle's pulling the trigger on his Sig Sauer automatic pistol, Oscar Grant's "left shoulder is up off the ground."

Rains took his theatrics further by calling Thomas Rogers, the forensic pathologist who performed the autopsy on Oscar Grant's body, in an attempt to prove that the shape of the bullet wound in Grant's back could only have been made because Grant was moving, i.e. 'resisting arrest,' with his 'shoulder coming up off the platform;' it didn't work. Rogers did identify the entry wound as being in the center of Oscar Grant's back and to the left of his spine but he did not co-sign Rains' primary assertion:

Rains: And in observing the entry wound that you've just described, what appearance did that wound have, sir?

Rogers: It was roughly ovoid in configuration ...

Rains: All right. And when you say that it is ovoid, what does that–what significance does that have, if any?

Rogers: It really to me, that's what its shape is. Beyond that, I don't attach a significance to it.

Rains: So you would not be able to say, for instance, indicate that the bullet entered the body from a certain angle?

Rogers: Sometimes, yes, but I deal with the angles on internal examination and follow the path. I think that's much more accurate than attempting to determine this from the shape of the entrance wound.

In summary it is neither credible, plausible nor common sense to believe that, because Oscar Grant was afraid of being returned to prison he: 1) waited until he was *underneath* the knee of Pirone, 2) with Johannes Mehserle on top of him from behind, 3) as he was pinned over the left leg of Carlos Reyes, 4) to attempt to avoid being arrested by Mehserle and Pirone by "wiggling away."

Oscar Grant was not murdered because he was "resisting arrest;" Oscar Grant was murdered due to the wanton chaos and recklessness of Anthony Pirone's and Johannes Mehserle's actions on Jan. 1, 2009.

7. Johannes Mehserle accidentally shot Oscar Grant with his service weapon when he meant to pull his taser

Johannes Mehserle intentionally shot Oscar Grant since, in his own words, he thought Grant was "going for a gun." This is what he stated the morning of Jan. 1, 2009, and subsequently thereafter.

David Mastagni, Mehserle's first attorney, handwrote that the shooting was intentional on the Breath Alcohol Test (BAT) form administered by the BART Authority when one of their officers is involved in a shooting. This is done to determine if an officer is under any chemical or alcohol influence. The BAT form must be signed by the officer to acknowledge that the test has been given. Johannes Mehserle undertook this test approximately four hours after murdering Oscar Grant and after consultation with Mastagni. The prosecution sought to have the BAT form allowed as evidence in the trial and stated their reasons why in their brief filed in court. The following paragraphs are taken from the district attorney's "Motion in Limine to Admit Breath Alcohol Form":

> In defendant's presence, Mr. Mastagni then spoke with BART Officer Ledford about the breath-alcohol testing procedure. In particular, Mr. Mastagni objected to the use of a department-issued form that referred to "post-accident" testing, and proposed that the language on the form be changed. Mr. Mastagni refused to allow defendant to participate in the test. Mr. Mastagni then met with BART Police Commander White and Lieutenant Alkire in a private office outside defendant's presence. Mr. Mastagni repeated his complaint that the language on the breath test form referred to the "post accident' nature of the testing. Mr. Mastagni said, *"This was not an accident. It was an intentional act."* [Emphasis mine].

That might have been enough but the prosecution continued their argument:

> The alcohol testing form … has a space marked "D: Reason for Test:" followed by several options with check boxes. "Post-Accident" is one of the boxes. After discussion, Mr. Mastagni agreed to allow defendant to take the test, and he and Commander White returned to defendant. In defendant's presence, Mr. Mastagni asked that Commander White order defendant to take the test. He also asked that the consent to testing form be changed to reflect that the testing was not consensual, but was done pursuant to order. The alcohol testing form was amended to add a handwritten option and checkbox: "Discharge of Firearm." The handwritten box is marked with a handwritten checkmark. The checkbox for "accident" was not marked. Defendant signed and initialed the form and thereafter completed the test.

The Alameda County D.A. felt the BAT form should be entered into evidence. Although Mehserle's consultation with Mastagni is protected under attorney-client privilege; their conversation would not have been revealed in court if Mastagni had been called to testify. The BAT form was not allowed into evidence at Mehserle's criminal trial in Los Angeles as Judge Perry ruled the form was inadmissible in the prosecution's case in chief, but could possibly be utilized if Mehserle testified. The prosecutor did not return to the issue of the BAT form.

Pirone testified that Mehserle stated to him that he thought Oscar Grant "was going for a gun." He repeated this same statement to other BART officers several minutes later. In the days that followed the murder of Oscar Grant, Mehserle's friend and fellow BART Officer Terry Foreman testified that Mehserle said "I thought he had a gun," and that Mehserle "would break down and start crying."

At *no time* did Mehserle ever mention to anyone that he accidentally shot Oscar Grant, or that he had meant to use his taser on Oscar Grant:

Stein: You stayed on that platform for about ten minutes; isn't that true?

Mehserle: Yes, sir.

Stein: And during your time on that platform did you ever feel the need to explain to anyone on the platform how Mr. Grant ended up being shot?

Mehserle: I was still trying to figure that out, sir.

Stein: Did you -- did you ever explain to anybody on that platform how this shooting took place?

Mehserle: No, sir.

Stein: You never told anyone it was an
              accident, did you?

Mehserle: No, sir.

Stein: You never told anyone that you meant
              to pull your taser, did you?

Mehserle: No, sir.

Stein: At any point during that ten-minute
              period where you remained on the
              platform did you ever radio for
              medical assistance?

Mehserle: Not that I remember, no, sir.

Stein: And after the shooting for that ten-
              minute period, did you ever use your
              radio to notify dispatch that there
              had been an officer-involved shooting?

Mehserle: I didn't, no, sir.

In his testimony in Los Angeles Mehserle was
adamant that he thought Oscar Grant was *going* for a
gun, even though he was not 100% certain that Oscar
Grant *actually* had a gun:

Stein: Now, you testified that when you
              observed what you believed Mr. Grant
              putting his hand in his right pocket,
              you believed at that time based on
              your prior experience that he was
              going for a gun; true?

Mehserle: It was the way in -- the way it led up

to that, yes.

Stein: What do you mean by that?

Mehserle: The -- like I said, he was keeping his
              hand from me. I was shouting -- or I
              was telling him commands. I was
              giving him commands, shouting
              commands. He just -- the effort that
              he -- that he used and the strength
              that he to keep his hands from me, I
              didn't know what his intentions were
              when his hands were in his front
              pocket and I'm pulling at it, telling
              him to give me his hand and he wasn't
              doing it, sir.

Stein: Could you see his pocket at that time?

Mehserle: I saw his hand digging in his pocket.

Stein: So that means you could see his
              pocket, true?

Mehserle: The image of his hand being inside of
              his pocket, that I don't -- I won't
              forget, but I can see his hand in his -- I
              can't see what's in his pocket, all I can
              see is his hand moving in his pocket.

Stein: Could you see his left hand at that
              time?

Mehserle: I was only focused on his right hand,
              sir.

Stein:	And it is your opinion or your belief that when you saw his hand going into his pocket, you believed at that time he was going for a gun; correct?
Mehserle:	I thought that I didn't want to get shot, sir. Yes, sir.
Stein:	And so you believed that he was going for a gun to use that gun against you and the other officers; is that right?
Mehserle:	I wasn't -- I thought he could be going for a gun. I wasn't -- I didn't see a gun.

Mehserle claims that he announced he was going to tase Oscar Grant, using the words "I'm going to tase him," so that Officer Pirone in particular would know what was about to happen. Mehserle did not however announce the word "gun," so that Officer Pirone would be aware of a potentially dangerous situation because, Mehserle said, he never actually saw a gun:

Stein:	Now, when you were standing in front of these young men, did you ever take the opportunity to at least visually inspect say their waistband or their pockets for bulges, things that could be weapons?
Mehserle:	It – I did a quick little glance, but I was more concerned with – I mean, I had done that, yes.
Stein:	You had done that?

Mehserle: Well, briefly. I mean, they were sitting down, so – I mean, I remember them having loose, baggy clothing and I don't – I didn't – I didn't notice – I didn't notice anything at that point in time.

Stein: As you sit there now do you recall looking for those things?

Mehserle: I like to think that I had. I don't remember specifically if I had or hadn't, but that's typically something I would do, yes, sir.

Stein: And at that point you say you believed he was going for a gun. You never said anything to anyone on that platform that you believed he was going for a gun at that time, did you?

Mehserle: I – I don't remember having any conversations on that platform.

Stein: You were trained that when you see a gun during the course of a search, you're supposed to yell "gun, gun, gun," correct?

Mehserle: Yes, sir.

Stein: What's your understanding as to why that's the case?

Mehserle: You want to alert the other officers in the area that there's a gun present.

Stein:	So if you really believed that he was going for a gun when you said his hand was in his pocket, why didn't you say, "I think he's going for a Gun. I think he's going for a gun"?
Mehserle:	I wasn't – I didn't see a gun, sir.
Stein:	I know you didn't see a gun, but you thought he was going for a gun, true?
Mehserle:	Yes, sir.
Stein:	Why did you not say to the other officers who were there, including officer Pirone, "I think he's going for a gun. I think he's going for a gun"?
Mehserle:	I gave him – I said, "I'm going to tase him. I'm going to tase him." That was – that's all that I was thinking, Sir.
Stein:	My question is why didn't you announce that you believed he was going for a gun?
Mehserle:	I didn't see a gun.
Stein:	So you're saying the reason why you didn't say it is because you didn't actually see a gun?
Mehserle:	Well, if I knew 100 percent that he had a gun, I would have yelled gun, yes, sir.
Stein:	So because you didn't see one,

> although you thought he was going
> for one, you felt "until I see a gun, I'm
> not going to announce gun," is that
> your testimony?

   ...   .

Mehserle: Yes sir.

How Mehserle could "see" Oscar Grant's hand going into his pocket as Grant is pinned underneath him, over the leg of Carlos Reyes, with Pirone on top of his head/neck, is beyond this writer's knowledge base. But I digress.

In those early morning hours of Jan. 1, 2009, Johannes Mehserle told no one that he had meant to use his taser but pulled his gun instead and shot Oscar Grant by accident. *He didn't even tell Oscar Grant that he had accidentally shot him, or that he meant to use his taser on him.* He did, however, handcuff Grant and perform a search to see if Grant had a gun. When queried on his reasons for handcuffing Oscar Grant Mehserle's replies were carefully worded to deflect away from any focus on his service weapon:

Stein: Did you call for medical assistance for Mr. Grant?

Mehserle: I don't – I mean, I know at this point that I didn't, no, sir.

Stein: You placed handcuffs on him, is that right?

Mehserle: Yes, sir.

Stein: And why did you place – at that time when you placed handcuffs on him, you knew you had shot him, right?

Mehserle: Yes, sir.

Stein: And what was your purpose for now putting handcuffs on him?

Mehserle: I remember him telling me – I remember telling him, "I need to put these handcuffs on you for just a second so I can search you." I searched him and then told him I'd take them right off. They weren't on there for – they were on there for a very short amount of time.

Stein: But you didn't need to handcuff him in order to search him, did you?

Mehserle: His hands were moving. I needed to be able to control his hands.

Stein: You have searched individuals before without handcuffing them, haven't you?

Mehserle: I had, yes, sir.

Stein: And this individual had just been shot in the back. Is there a reason why he needed to be handcuffed before you searched him?

Mehserle: I just needed to make sure – I needed

– I hadn't search him, so I needed to make sure that I had searched him, and then I took the handcuffs off immediately after I eliminated the possibility that he had anything – any gun or anything like that.

Stein: Did you feel at that time after you had shot him that he still posed a lethal threat to you?

Mehserle: I hadn't searched him so I – it was still – I think after – it took a second for it to set in because I was just confused on what just happened.

Stein: Did you still believe that he posed a lethal threat to you after you shot him?

Mehserle: I needed to make sure to search him so he didn't – so I could eliminate that possibility.

Stein: So at that point in time it was still a possibility in your mind, correct?

Mehserle: He was still moving. I hadn't searched him, yes, sir.

Stein: Then why did you put your gun away?

Mehserle: Because I didn't – I never intended to shoot him.

Stein: But you still – you said it was a possibility he still posed a lethal threat to you. Why did you put your gun away?

Mehserle: My gun was never supposed to be out. I just put it away.

Stein: Aren't you supposed to have your gun out when you're threatened with lethal force?

Mehserle: Yeah, I didn't mean – this is not what I intended to do.

Stein: But you said that you believed he still posed a lethal threat to you, true?

Mehserle: At that point in time, I just needed to eliminate that possibility. I don't – I probably wasn't thinking very clear after that.

Stein: So you put handcuffs on him?

Mehserle: For a second. I told him I'd take them right off.

Stein: Did anyone tell you to put handcuffs on him?

Mehserle: No.

. . .　　. . .　　　. . .

Stein: Did you ever feel the need to tell Mr. Grant that you shot him by accident?

Mehserle: I told him he'd be okay. I just needed him to calm down.

Stein:	To calm down?
Mehserle:	Because I didn't – like I said, he was hysterical.
Stein:	When you say he was hysterical, what was he saying or doing at that time?
Mehserle:	He said that – I remember, you know, "you shot me." He was looking up at me and – and he was moving around a lot. I told him, "you'll be all right. Just you need to calm down. You'll be all right. You'll be all right."
Stein:	Did you ever see the need to explain to him that you had fired your gun by accident?
Mehserle:	I was just thinking about him at that point making sure, get him CALMED down. [emphasis in original transcript].
Stein:	You never told him that you shot him by accident, did you?
Mehserle:	I don't remember, no, sir.
Stein:	You never told him that you meant to tase him, did you?
Mehserle:	No, I don't think I did, sir.
Stein:	And then about two minutes after you shot Mr. Grant, you approached officer Pirone and you told him "Tony, I thought he was going for a gun," isn't

that right?

Mehserle: I don't – after that I remember seeing faces, and the only faces that I remember seeing were just angry faces looking at me. But talking to – I don't – I don't remember having any contact with Pirone, sir.

Stein: You recall him testifying at the preliminary hearing and at this trial that at the ... southern end of the platform closer to the train operator, you approached him and you said the words, "Tony, I thought he was going for a gun." Do you recall that testimony by officer Pirone?

Mehserle: I remember the testimony.

It is not unusual for a defendant in a trial to go over his/her testimony with their attorney prior to taking the stand. Mehserle's testimony in Los Angeles however revealed something other than a defendant who was "well prepared;" his testimony revealed that it was rehearsed – memorized – focusing away from pulling his gun and on his lie of "taser confusion" and its justification, to the point that his answers neither made any sense nor did they fit the questions posed to him by the prosecutor. I have quoted extensively from the court transcript to illustrate this point:

Stein: Another thing you were trained with regard to taser use had to do with involuntary reflexes; is that correct?

Mehserle: I don't – I'm not very familiar with that term.

Stein: Let's see if we can refresh your recollection. … I'm going to show you a clip from the DVD that you were shown during your taser training regarding involuntary reflexes, and let me ask you to watch it and see if this refreshes your memory.

        …   …   …

Stein: Showing you that clip, does that refresh your recollection as to what you were taught about involuntary reflexes?

Mehserle: I don't remember the clip specifically, but I could have.

        …   …   …

Stein: You do recall being taught about involuntary reflexes, correct?

Mehserle: It's possible that it was a subject on there. I mean, now I don't remember specifically everything that we were taught as far as that goes.

Stein: Do you remember being taught that when the taser probes hit the subject, that there's a muscle restrict? You knew that; right?

Mehserle: Yes, sir.

Stein: That's what happened to you when you were tased, correct, your muscles got real tense, correct?

Mehserle: I think so.

Stein: And in this – you think so?

Mehserle: Well, some people I guess react to it a little bit different.

Stein: Do you recall being trained that when the taser is applied to a subject, the subject's muscles will constrict?

Mehserle: Yes, sir.

Stein: Okay. And in this video did you see the person's hands constrict and go up on their feet? Did you see that?

Mehserle: I did, yes, sir.

Stein: Now, knowing that, having that knowledge, why would you want to cause a hand that's around a gun to constrict when you are trying to get that gun away from them? Wouldn't that pose a danger to everybody in the area?

Mehserle: I didn't – that wasn't something that I considered.

Stein: You would agree now though that if there was a gun in that pocket, that by using a taser it could cause that gun to involuntarily discharge; right?

Mehserle: I'm not sure.

There were times when Mehserle's answers seemed akin to trying to force a series of square pegs into round holes:

Stein: Tell me, isn't it consistent with training that if you see someone in the circumstances that you were in going for a gun, that the last thing you would want to do is to pull that gun in that hand out of the pocket?

Mehserle: I had – no, I had – as I was pulling on his hand and he wasn't giving me his hand, his hand was still in his pocket, I had let go, I had made the announcement, I said I was going to tase him, and I stepped back –

Stein: I'm talking –

Mehserle: – to tase him.

Stein: Go ahead.

Mehserle: Go ahead.

Stein: I'm talking about the time that you saw the hand go into the pocket and you were pulling it out. You said at that time you believed he was going for a gun while you were pulling it out.

Mehserle: It took a few tugs just to kind of set in for me to make that decision. It was –

Stein: Wouldn't you agree that the last thing you'd really want to do is to actually pull the gun out with his hand on it? He could shoot you or anybody there; correct?

Mehserle: Yes, sir.

Stein: How much did you weigh that night?

Mehserle: Probably around 250 pounds, sir.

Stein: How much did it look like [Oscar Grant] weighed?

Mehserle: Maybe 160, 170 pounds, sir.

Stein: If you really thought that he was going for a gun, wouldn't it have been consistent with your training to keep that gun and that hand in that pocket underneath him so that he couldn't do anything?

Mehserle: I felt that at that time the taser would have been the best tool to use at that time to keep – to immobilize him so that way I wasn't   if he did pull a gun I wasn't rolling around with him struggling with it, you know.

Stein: But you were pulling that gun out of his pocket?

Mehserle: I was trying to pull his hand out of that pocket, sir.

Stein: And you believed that hand was around

a gun, correct?

Mehserle: I wasn't sure, sir.

Stein: But you believed that it was?

Mehserle: It was possible.

Stein: In order to use the taser the way you said you were trying to use it, you created distance between Mr. Grant and the gun and where you were, did you not?

Mehserle: Yes, sir.

Stein: If you believed that he was actually going for a gun, why would you create distance between you and the threat?

Mehserle: Because I know I needed to make distance for that taser to work.

Stein: But in the time it took you to give distance for that taser to work, couldn't he have just spun around and shot you?

Mehserle: Now that I think about it, that's a possibility, yes, sir.

Mehserle's reaction immediately after shooting Oscar Grant in the back, the look of shock on his face, was due to his having realized that he had just shot an unarmed man – *not* that he had pulled his service weapon instead of his taser.

Johannes Mehserle would never have spent one night in jail had his defense team not been so adamant about pushing the vile and vulgar damn lie of taser confusion. When a white police officer shoots a person of Afrikan descent in the U.S. and proclaims "I thought he had a gun," it is an automatic "Get out of Jail Free Card."

It always has been.

CHAPTER THREE

The keyboard is mightier than the sword

"Oscar Grant was murdered for the first time on Jan. 1, 2009, and he has been murdered every day since then in the media."
~ Thandisizwe Chimurenga, October 22, 2010

Oscar Grant was treated more like a suspect than a victim in mainstream media. This mistreatment, which sometimes occurred under the guise of reporting the facts, led up to the trial of his murderer Johannes Mehserle and has lasted well after it. The libeling of Oscar Grant and the lies published about him have been pounced upon by supporters of Mehserle in particular and law enforcement personnel in general as truth and evidence that Oscar Grant was responsible for his own death and not Johannes Mehserle. The reportage of pieces of Oscar Grant's life and what happened on the Fruitvale BART platform that New Year's morning, as well as comments made by consumers on the news websites and on various social media sites (see screenshots at end of chapter) are how we can best document the third murder of Oscar Grant.

Although the official name of the trial was People of the State of California, Plaintiff v. Johannes Mehserle, Defendant, Demian Bulwa's May 30, 2010, article in the *San Francisco Chronicle* was correct when the headline proclaimed *"Oscar Grant's Character, Shooter Both on Trial."* Published more than one year after Oscar's murder, the article attempted to show Oscar from the point of view of family and friends at the same time that it talked about his run-ins with the law, and the decision of Judge Perry to allow aspects of Oscar's past history to be presented to the jury. No such mention was made of any errors or miss-steps in Johannes Mehserle's background in this article. As a matter of fact, Johannes Mehserle wasn't even mentioned by name in the headline; only by implication, and it was he, not Oscar Grant, who was supposed to be on trial.

The electronic version of Bulwa's article on the *Chronicle's* website (SFGate.com) racked up a total of 378 comments as of this writing; of these, the majority of them call Oscar a thug, a criminal, *or* call him a thug and a criminal and blame him for his own death. Despite this, the murder by media of Oscar Grant actually began not long after Johannes Mehserle pulled the trigger of his .40 caliber Sig Sauer.

A study of viewer comments on the videos of Oscar's murder uploaded to YouTube covered the month immediately following the incident – January 1, 2009 – through Feb. 2, 2009. "This is Citizen Journalism at its Finest: YouTube and the Public Sphere in the Oscar Grant Shooting Incident," was published in the journal *New Media and Society* by Mary Grace Antony and Ryan J. Thomas. The authors, then-doctoral students in the Edward R. Murrow College of Communication at Washington State University, sought to examine comments from people regarding "non-media individuals … ordinary citizens documenting, in their words, unjust and unwarranted aggression against an unarmed man."

Antony and Thomas chose to examine uploaded video footage from non-professionals and studied a percentage of the total comments from four different videos. While the authors noted viewers' critique of the quality of the videos, the camerapersons' ('witnesses') presence of mind to record the event as it unfolded, etc., the authors also noticed something else – the presence of "inflammatory and derogatory comments."

This aspect of the viewers' comments was not supposed to be a part of the study but it troubled the authors enough for them to make mention of it stating, "It was indeed disheartening to note the excessive presence of racial slurs, outright insults and other provocative reactions *that comprised the majority of all posted comments.*" [Emphasis mine].

Several videos of the shooting from various angles and sources have made their way onto the internet; three of them, uploaded to YouTube within days of the murder, have amassed more than 3 million views and close to 20,000 comments. Although YouTube has a scrolling feature to view the comments, they start with the most recent ones and there is no mechanism to automatically view the first comments made about the videos. The sheer viciousness of white supremacist commentary was too sickening to attempt to wade through until reaching the very beginning for the purposes of this chapter, but the work of Antony and Thomas can be seen as representative of the predominant tone.

Most journalists attempt to "do no harm" to the subjects they report on however harm was caused to Oscar Grant since this reporting lacked context and/or probing questions, even though factually accurate information was relayed to the public. There was no "basic skepticism" to accompany the reporting. The harm caused by this may have been unintentional but it happened nonetheless. The publication of Johannes Mehserle's motion for bail provides a case in point.

Michael Rains submitted his motion asking that his client be released on bail to the court on Jan. 30, 2009. This document, as in most of the documents related to the trial, was made available to the public and members of the press scooped them up. The *San Francisco Chronicle*, the *Oakland Tribune* and several other news organizations as well as the Associated Press (AP) wire service reported on the details of the bail motion, and many news organizations also made PDFs of the motion available to the public in an attempt to provide source material directly to news consumers.

Rains began his motion for bail with a flowery characterization of Johannes Mehserle's life ("he was voted Most Huggable in High School"), and then went on to describe Oscar Grant as "the alleged victim." Rains then states the following:

> It has been reported, (but not confirmed through discovery provided to the defense to date) that Grant had been convicted of drug dealing and was sentenced to 16 months in state prison in 2007 after he fled from a traffic stop while armed with a loaded pistol. Grant had been released from prison September 23, 2008. Toxicology testing of Oscar Grant's blood revealed the presence of alcohol 0.02 grams and the presence of the drug Fentanyl.

Fentanyl is described as a highly addictive, strong narcotic pain reliever.

At the time of the bail motion and the reporting on it, Rains described Oscar Grant's criminal background as being "reported but not confirmed." While it may be acceptable to mention this in a court of law the question must be asked why it was acceptable to print something that was "reported but not confirmed" in a newspaper or on a news website? This reporting was factually accurate insofar as it repeated the contents of the bail motion, but independent verification of the contents of the bail motion – the existence of and specifics of Oscar's criminal background – were not done at the time this was reported.

The journalists who reported on the bail motion quoted from the document verbatim; there was no chance for error through misquoting in most of the reports since, as mentioned above, many of the news organizations also made a copy of the document available on their own news sites. The main problem was to be found in the lack of context for the reporting of the "facts."

The comments sections of print, radio and television news websites are, understandably, often written off as cess pools of vile and vulgar anomalies (racism, homophobia, misogyny, ableism, classism, etc. and so on). But these areas also provide a wealth of knowledge regarding consumers' points of view on the subjects at hand. They can also be seen as an echo chamber and a "temperature check," especially in regards to the areas of public policy and support for law enforcement. It is here in the comments sections that we find some of the most racist and despicable attacks on Oscar Grant.

A favorite attack hurled against Oscar by supporters of Mehserle (in particular and law enforcement in general) was that Oscar Grant was high on drugs and that he had been drinking at the time of his death. This libel is a result of the reportage referring to the presence of Fentanyl in Oscar Grant's system and its description as "a strong narcotic." Although the legal blood alcohol limit in the State of California is .08 percent, the presence of .02 percent alcohol in Oscar's system was seized upon as an example of a parolee being in violation of his parole conditions. While prohibition of alcohol is a rather common condition of parole in California and elsewhere, Oscar Grant's explicit parole prohibitions are unknown. Illegal drugs on the other hand are always prohibited.

As both a reporter and observer of Mehserle's trial the issue of the Fentanyl in Oscar's system troubled me from the beginning. Although I have never been a connoisseur of illicit or illegal drugs I was still bothered by the fact that I had never, *ever*, heard of this drug. How was it that this 22-year old Black youth had come into contact with it? According to news reports (confirmed?) Grant had been convicted of possessing Ecstasy with intent to sell. Of course it was entirely plausible that he could have gotten the Fentanyl from the same place he had gotten the Ecstasy; yet I continued to have doubts. Call it a reporter's hunch. I asked various sources had they ever heard of the drug Fentanyl? Did it have a street name? Fentanyl has been cited as being similar (though *not* exact) to heroin and morphine. Were heroin and morphine in demand enough for a 22-year old from Hayward to sell them? Were they making a comeback? My inquiries returned no leads.

Just prior to Mehserle's trial for murder, I learned that the Fentanyl was present in Oscar Grant's system because it's what the doctors at Highland Hospital administered to him as they tried to save his life. It was Michael Rains himself who stated it during a May 7, 2010, pretrial hearing in Los Angeles in reference to Oscar's toxicology report:

> " … Five hours later the blood draw occurs, and it occurs post-surgically I might add which is why if you remember that toxicology report there was also Fentanyl found in the blood. And Fentanyl, as it turns out, was administered to Mr. Grant post-surgically to reduce pain. That's why that blood sample had Fentanyl."

Since a gag order had been imposed in the case after the publication of Rains' motion for bail – which broached the subject of the "strong narcotic pain reliever" in the first place – there was no way Rains could right the libeling of Oscar Grant by making an announcement to the press. None of the news organizations that reported that Oscar had Fentanyl in his system (via the motion for bail) did a follow-up – or a correction – announcing Rains' statement, one year and three months later.

The reader is also urged to take note that the article in which Oscar Grant's family and friends talked about him turning his life around also did not appear until one year and three months after publication of the bail motion's contents. The damage had already been done.

If just *one* reporter would have asked the question(s) what is Fentanyl and how is it available to a 22-year old Black youth in Hayward, California, *maybe* it would have led to other questions, and deeper probing of the other charges leveled against Oscar Grant's character in Rains' motion. Had questions been asked and assumptions not been made, *maybe* Oscar Grant would not have been considered a "criminal," "thug," and a "scumbag" who was "high on drugs" and "fighting," and "causing trouble" on BART, and thus responsible for his own death.

The murder of Oscar Grant through the media continued with the attention given to redeem his murderer via a prime time television interview. Just prior to Mehserle's formal sentencing on Nov. 5, 2010, Bay Area television station KTVU presented an exclusive interview of Johannes Mehserle from the L.A. County Jail during the week of Oct. 25, 2010, and aired segments of it over a period of three-to-four days. It was the first time since Oscar's murder on Jan. 1, 2009, that Mehserle had spoken about the crime to anyone other than family, close friends or his legal team. In an attempt to be "balanced," KTVU also gave air-time to Oscar Grant's family via a KTVU interview, however, we should all agree that's not quite the same thing as having Oscar speak for himself. Veteran journalist Rita Williams conducted the interview of Johannes Mehserle stating, "You might say I have been working on getting an interview with [him] since the shooting, trying to be fair and balanced in my reporting."

In his book *Just the Facts: How 'Objectivity' Came To*

Define American Journalism, David Mindich, professor at Vermont's Saint Michael's College, asks the question, "… how does one balance a story about lynching?" Mindich devotes an entire chapter to the necessary journalism of Ida B. Wells and how her work was correct in its assessment that lynching was a savage and racist crime against Black people, despite attacks on Wells' claims (and her character) from media such as the *New York Times*. Police murder is also a savage and racist crime against Black people, but most media outlets continue to promote the cruel myth that "fair and balanced" reporting is needed on the issue.

Activists seeking justice for Oscar Grant denounced KTVU's airing of Mehserle's interview, saying it was a public relations stunt that was designed to create sympathy for Mehserle the week before his sentencing for Involuntary Manslaughter. Williams offered many self-serving questions during the interview, such as, "Some people see you as a racist; are you? A cold-blooded killer?"

Mehserle basically stuck to his courtroom testimony script for this interview, making sure to state that he never "intended" to shoot Oscar Grant on Jan. 1, 2009. Writing for *Colorlines*, Julianne Hing said Mehserle was playing to his strengths, noting that he was "…a young guy with baby cheeks and sloping shoulders and a demeanor that's entirely non-threatening. He hasn't got a sharp angle to his face and he's trained himself to look up at the ceiling between sentences, which he frequently punctuates with "ma'am" and "sir." He doesn't fit the classic profile of a brutal cop and he knows it."

Mehserle's white supremacist leanings crept through the interview, however, when he stated "I didn't expect to walk through those doors in handcuffs ... I didn't think I'd be convicted at all." Such are the delusions that privilege provides.

While Los Angeles and the Bay Area of Northern California awaited the verdict in Johannes Mehserle's trial, the rest of the country had other things on its mind: not justice for Oscar Grant, or the specter and fear and loathing of a possible "riot" and property damage following an unjust verdict, but on Lebron James' announcement that he would be leaving the Cleveland Cavaliers basketball team to play in Miami.

Or so the media reported.

A

sampling

of

the

Old and New Media

murder

of

Oscar Grant

Following the San Francisco Chronicle's publication of the contents of Mehserle's motion for bail on Jan. 30, 2009:

qawagstaff: *"Mr.Grant shouldn't have been shot but he wasn't the angel portrayed. A convicted felon resisting arrest. It is a very sad and tragic accident."*

residentevil98: *"one less thug in the world."*

residentevil9: "If Oscar Grant was such a devoted father what the hell was he doing out at 2 am. Why wasn't he at home with his daughter. Instead he was out looking for trouble. What a loser. That is why he has a criminal record."

getreal_1: "These thugs were fighting & unruly on the train. Its obvious in the video that they were resisting an officer and arrest. Hello?! . When an officer tells you to follow instructions-do it! Duh. Johannes will be found not guilty, but I'm sure the family will get their $$ just like Burris."

Following the San Francisco Chronicle's publication of Demian Bulwa's piece entitled "Grant's Character, Shooter, on Trial" on May 30, 2010:

BigSquash: *"Maybe the idea behind presenting Grant as a loving father "trying to turn his life around", instead of as the thug he was, is to help incite violence when Mehserle is acquitted .. More violence means more stories to report.*

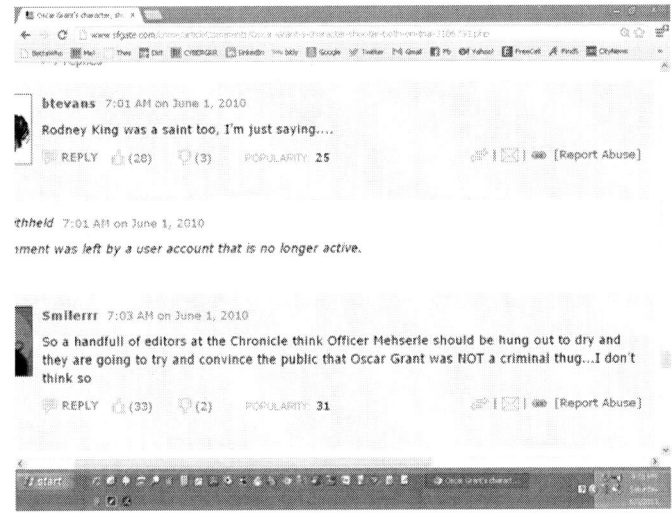

Preceding Page:

Prior to the start of Mehserle's criminal trial in Los Angeles, from the SF Chronicle's website:

btevans: *"Rodney King was a saint too. I'm just saying ..."*

Smilerrr: *"So a handful of editors at the Chronicle think Officer Mehserle should be hung out to dry and they are going to try and convince the public that Oscar Grant was NOT a criminal thug ... I don't think so."*

sanity4achange: *"Vid., where are you getting that he was handcuffed and restrained already? Both Mehserle and Pirone state that he was struggling and resisting while he was trying to handcuf him. So...the fact that he was intoxicated, if he was, would be relevant especially if he was extremely intoxicated because you tend to get even more belligerent with authority. That is why his toxicology report could be relevant."*

Ginger28: *"In the motion for bail, Rains cited that the autopsy showed that Grant had a blood alcohol levelof 0.02% and was high on Fentanyl - - used for cancer patients, which is 100 times stronger than Morphine. It is often illegally used by people to achieve a high similar to that of heroin."*

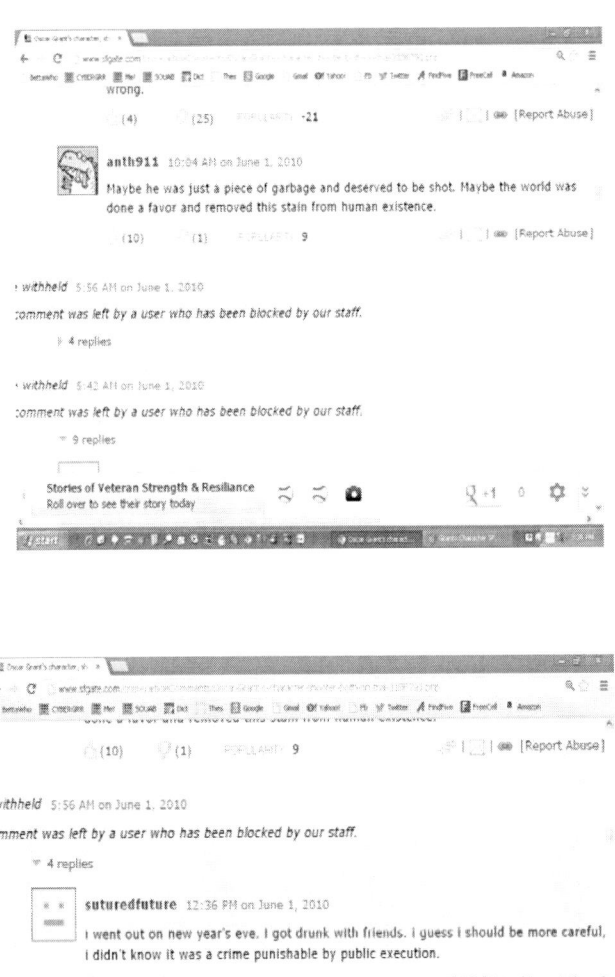

Preceding Page:

anth911: *"Maybe he was just a piece of garbage and deserved to be shot. Maybe the world was done a favor and removed this stain from human existence."*

suturedfuture: *"I went out on new year's eve. I got drunk with friends. I guess I should be more careful, I didn't know it was a crime punishable by public execution."*

sfrealitycheck: *"suturedfuture --- did you also try to pick fights with strangers, scream obscenities, and violently resist arrest (as opposed to calmly cooperating) with the police?"*

From the Facebook group Free Johannes Mehserle, following Mehserle's conviction for Involuntary Manslaughter in the murder of Oscar Grant:

Kevin Truong*: "This is a disgrace ... You don't put your hands up like the police officer says, but instead you uput your hands in your fucking pocket. So naurally, you would be tazed. But he accidently, the keyword is ACCIDENTLY, took out his gun and shot hi. To be honest, Oscar Grant actually deserved to be shot... So shame on you fucking Oakland and Shame on you LA."*

From the Facebook group BART Police Officer Johannes Mehserle Is Just Innocent, following Mehserle's sentencing to two years in state prison for Involuntary Manslaughter:

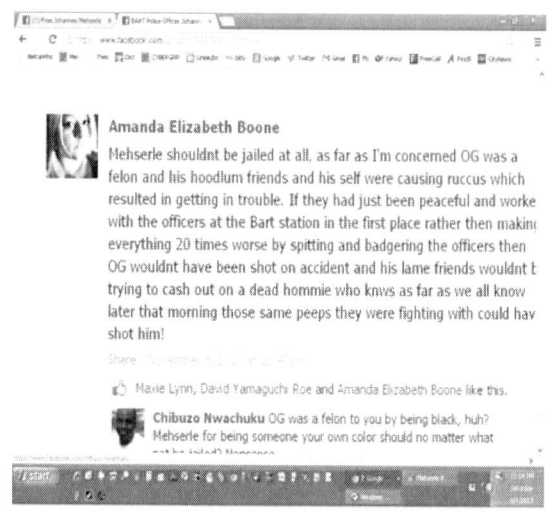

Amanda Elizabeth Boone: *"Mehserle shouldnt be jailed at all, as far as I'm concerned OG was a felon and his hoodlum friends and his self were causing ruccus which resulted in getting in trouble. If they had just been peaceful and worked with the officers at the Bart station in the first place rather than making everything 20 times worse by spitting and badgering the officers then OG wouldnt have been shot on accident and his lame friends wouldnt be trying to cash out on a dead hommie who knws as far as we all know later that morning those same peeps they were fighting with could have shot him!"*

From the Facebook group BART Police Officer Johannes Mehserle Is Just Innocent:

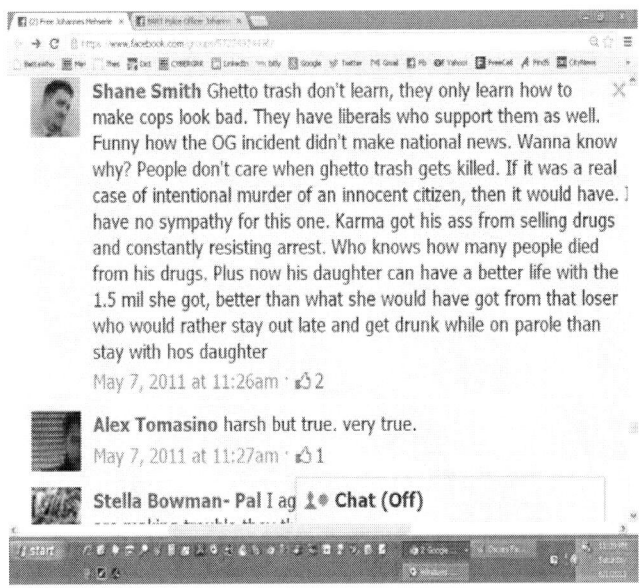

Shane Smith: "*Ghetto trash don't learn, they only learn how to make cops look bad. They have liberals who support them as well. Funny how the OG incident didn't make national news. If it was a real case of intentional murder of an innocent citizen, then it would have. I have no sympathy for this one. Karma got his ass from selling drugs and constantly resisting arrest. Who knows how many people died from his drugs. Plus now his daughter can have a better life with the 1.5 mil she got, better than what she would have got from that loser who would rather stay out late and get drunk while on parole than stay with hos daughter*"

From the Facebook group "Johannes Mehserle Is Just Innocent," following the acquittal of Mehserle and four other BART officers on charges of excessive force in the assault of Kenneth Carrethers, Dec. 1, 2011. Todd Mehserle is the father of Johannes Mehserle, murderer of Oscar Grant:

Todd Mehserle: "In effect, Oscar Grants family murdered him by lack of raising a kid to a higher standard. Uncle Bobby's remorse (that he should have) is all about abandonment and not being the big brother he should have been to his sisterd kid whose father, to this day, sis in S.Q., life with no parole.... ever hear an apology from that family who certainly through murder and drug dealing has altered countless lives?"

Todd Mehserle: "we should waste anymore time on them ... a prayer maybe in hopes they see the light."

From the Facebook group BART Police Officer Johannes Mehserle Is Just Innocent:

Todd Mehserle's opinion on Justice for Oscar Grant:

'Tis the Season … GO SHARKS !!!

From the Facebook group Free Johannes Mehserle: Oscar Grant's name placed inside of toilet bowl, at the spot where the "waste would hit." The "UB" referred to is Cephus Johnson, Oscar's "Uncle Bobby". One commenter suggests switching Oscar's name with Uncle Bobby's. Todd is the father of Johannes Mehserle. "OG lovers" refers to the supporters of Justice for Oscar Grant.

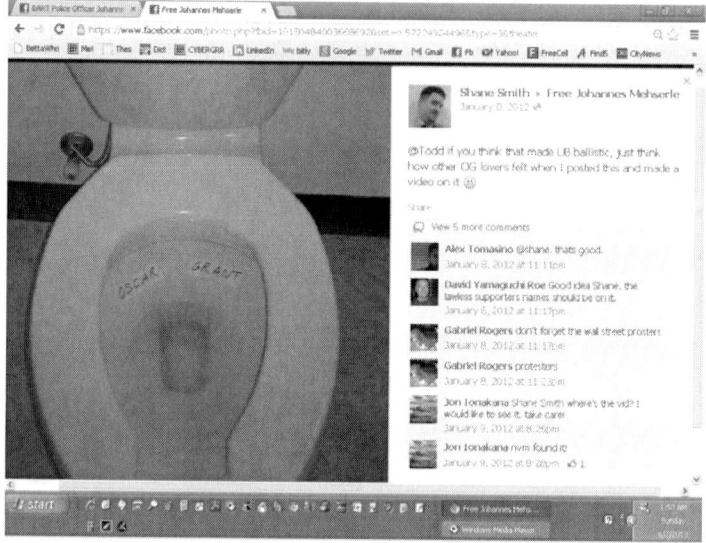

Shane Smith: "@Todd if you think that made UB ballistic, just think how other OG lovers felt when I posted this and made a video on it"

Shane Smith: "I got the idea from a comment on the SF article about naming a trash can after him. I was going to name the toilet after him, but that would be an insult to the toilet, so I made his name where my waste would hit."

The author ends both comments with a smiley face.

Calguns dot net is a pro law enforcement, pro 2nd amendment site.

Preceding Page:

Rouge Recon: *"If Grant was an upstanding citizen, he would still be alive today. Period."*

Funbaby: *"At a bbq recently, I was chatting to one of the lawyers involved in the Oscar Grant case. His personal opinion was that the deceased was alow life petty criminal. Nuff said."*

Chimpout," a notorious white supremacist internet site, regarding the announcment of a movie on Oscar Grant, in August, 2012:

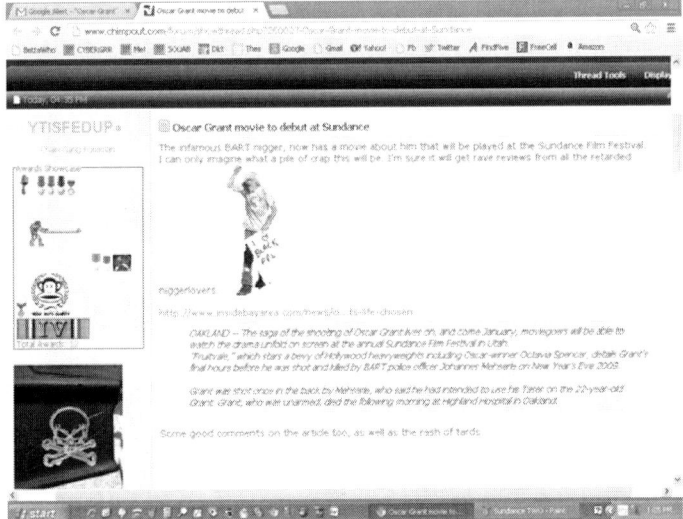

YTISFEDUP: *"The infamous BART nigger, now has a movie about him that will be played at the Sundance Film Festival. I can only imagine what a pile of crap this will be. I'm sure it will get rave reviews from all the retarded niggerlovers."*

THANDISIZWE CHIMURENGA

From the SF Chronicle, upon Mehserle's release from the L.A. County jail:

martin175c: *"Let's get some things strait. Oscar Grant was not the smiley-faced, angel depicted on posters and tee-shirts. He was a thug with a criminal record. He's been sentenced to prison and he has had multiple arrests. He's had a history of resisting arrests. He and his gang-banging, thug friends were fighting with others on BART which led to the unfortunate events of that night. I am not saying he deserved what happened to him, but had he been behaving like a normal human being, he would still be alive today.*

What happened to him was a terrible ACCIDENT. The case has been debated to death (excuse the pun). The prosecution could NOT prove that Mehserle murdered Grant and Mehserle did his time. The only thing Mehserle is guilty of is stupidity and inexperience.

The take-away from all this should be to stay-out of trouble period. If I were to ever brawl in a public place, I would expect the police to show up and arrest me. Furthermore, if I were to then physically resist arrest, I would expect to be physically subdued and possibly shot.

Let's be clear. This is NOT justification for killing a man (last sentence first paragraph). All I'm saying is this could have been avoided had Grant not acted like such a thug that night. This could also have been avoided had Mehserle looked to confirm that he was pulling his taser and not his gun!

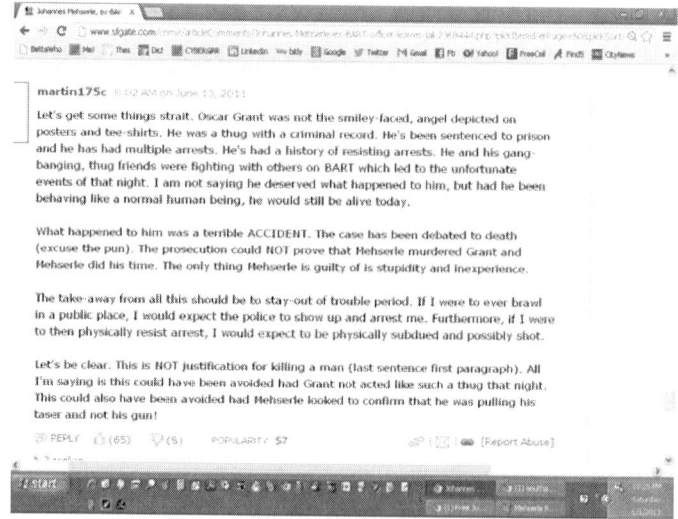

CHAPTER FOUR

Legalese or Legal Ease?

"My son was murdered. He was murdered. He was murdered. He was murdered."
~ Wanda Johnson, mother of Oscar Grant, July 8, 2010

All of us, every last one of us, has been conditioned to look for (and believe in) justice through the United States legal system. That sounds like an obvious and sensible proposition but the laws and structures of the U.S. legal system appear to be anything but to the average person who does not have the benefit of legal training. "When we talk about these [jury] instructions, there's good news and bad news," said prosecutor Stein in closing arguments. "Okay. The good news is they're based on common sense, right? There's really no magic to them. The bad news is they were written by lawyers and so they tend to be wordy. They tend to sound like they have a lot of legal jargon."

Well, they do have a lot of legal jargon. The question becomes one of who such jargon is meant to serve?

California's Penal Code defines 'murder' as "the unlawful killing of a human being … with malice aforethought." It goes on to state the two types of "malice aforethought," which prosecutor Stein also reiterated in the courtroom:

> Such malice may be express or
> implied. It is express when there is

manifested a deliberate intention unlawfully to take away the life of a fellow human. It is implied when no considerable provocation appears, or when the circumstances attending the killing show an abandoned and malignant heart. When it is shown that the killing resulted from the intentional doing of an act with express or implied malice as defined above, no other mental state need be shown to establish the mental state of malice aforethought.

In other words, for malice aforethought to be an express factor, a person does not have to know the victim beforehand; a person does not have to know the victim and then develop hatred in their heart for the victim or simply have hatred. The "deliberate intention to unlawfully take away the life" of a person is sufficient enough to show express malice.

For implied malice, simply not caring or having "an abandoned or malignant heart" is sufficient.

A warrant for the arrest of Johannes Mehserle was signed January 13, 2009, for the crime of murder, but the degree of murder was omitted. Then-Alameda County District Attorney Tom Orloff said he made the decision to charge Mehserle with murder, in part because Grant was unarmed, subdued and his hands were behind his back at the time Mehserle shot him and that Mehserle, Orloff said, shot Grant in "an intentional, unlawful act:

When you basically have a situation of an

NO DOUBT: THE MURDER(S) OF OSCAR GRANT

unlawful, intentional killing of one
individual by another, and that's all you
know – and that's really all we know in
this case – then that's a murder.

Orloff went on to state that, based on the
evidence he had thus far, he didn't see anything "that
would mitigate that to something lower than a
murder." To my knowledge, Orloff never
acknowledged what impact the rebellion in the streets
of Oakland had on his decision to charge Mehserle
with murder.

Section 189 of California's penal code lists
several determinants for a charge of murder in the
first degree:

All murder which is perpetrated by
means of destructive device or
explosive; a weapon of mass
destruction; knowing use of
ammunition designed primarily to
penetrate metal or armor; poison;
lying in wait; *torture*; or by any other
kind of willful, deliberate and
premeditated killing, or which is
committed in the perpetration of, or
attempt to perpetrate: arson, rape,
carjacking, robbery, burglary, *mayhem*,
kidnapping, train wrecking … or, any
murder which is perpetrated by means
of discharging a firearm from a motor
vehicle, intentionally at another person
outside of the vehicle with the intent
to inflict death, is murder of the first
degree. [Emphasis mine].

Felony murder, "the unlawful killing of a human being under circumstances that amount to a felony crime" – such as torture or mayhem – is classified as murder in the First Degree. In plain old everyday language, a felony is considered to be a "serious crime" with punishment being more "severe" than the type of punishment meted out for a "misdemeanor." Mark Cabaniss, an Orange County-based attorney who has worked as both a prosecutor and a public defender, cites the following hypothetical situation as an example to further illustrate felony first degree murder:

> You have kidnapped someone. You don't want to hurt him — you merely want the ransom money. While you are driving down the road, the victim is bound and blindfolded in the back seat of your car. Somehow, he gets the door open and jumps out while the car is going 50 miles an hour. He dies. You are guilty of felony murder because the death arose out of your felony — kidnapping, which is a dangerous crime. You are not merely guilty of murder; you are guilty of first-degree murder. Your lawyer isn't even allowed to argue that there is no evidence of intent to kill; the judge won't let him, because such evidence is irrelevant.

Cabaniss cites the actual 2006 California case of People V. Wilkins as another example:

> a burglar was driving away with stolen
> goods when some of them fell off the
> truck onto the roadway, causing the
> driver behind the burglar to swerve,
> wreck, and die. The burglar was
> convicted of first-degree felony
> murder because the death was caused
> by the commission of his felony —
> burglary.

Convicted by a jury of Involuntary Manslaughter on July 8, 2010, in the murder of Oscar Grant, Felony First Degree Murder was the more apt charge to apply to Johannes Mehserle's actions. Under a white supremacist system however, no prosecutor, no judge and no jury would have been comfortable in convicting a white, (former) police officer of such a charge.

Probably because it contains the word "slaughter" in it, "manslaughter" has always sounded to me like a frightening, dreadful and very, very bad thing. It is, but in the legal sense, it is not as bad – not as heinous – as murder, which is why the penalties for these offenses differ. Manslaughter in simple terms means to kill someone unlawfully (unjustifiably); but if the act of killing someone was "voluntary," that means the person was in control of their faculties (or circumstances) but there was something else going on at the time – the person was "provoked into it", or it was "in the heat of passion." The killing would be mitigated but *not excused*.

If the killing, which was unlawful, happened without any intent to kill, this form of manslaughter is known as "involuntary," meaning the person was not necessarily in control of their faculties or their circumstances. This would mean that the person was doing a bad thing – driving drunk (which is also against the law, by the way) and they hit someone and killed them. The driver had no qualms at all about speeding; they had no qualms at all about driving while drunk, but they never *meant* to kill anyone. In other words, it was an accident kinda but not quite: the law is clear that the perpetrator must still be held accountable for the crime.

The defense's position, as measured by commentary on both news and social media sites, by the supporters of Johannes Mehserle – whether they actually knew him or not – was that since Mehserle committed an accident, albeit a tragic one, he should not be subjected to the criminal justice system via trial, let alone face any jail time. Many of Mehserle's supporters expressed actual *anger* that legal charges were brought against him. As stated above, from a legal standpoint accidental killings may have a mitigating factor *but they are not excused.* The only logical conclusion to the vitriol coming from Mehserle's supporters is that, under white supremacy, a white police officer should *never, ever* be held accountable and subject to punishment for the death of a young Black man.

The Los Angeles jury's conviction of Johannes Mehserle for Involuntary Manslaughter in the murder of Oscar Grant was basically its way of saying, 1) Mehserle meant/did intend to pull his weapon and shoot Oscar Grant, but 2) he did not intend to kill Oscar Grant. This finding by the jury rejected the defense's damn lie that Mehserle was going for his taser but grabbed his gun instead, but it still affirmed the prevailing notion that Mehserle could not have possibly *intended to purposely* kill Grant because the shooting happened out in the open with too many witnesses around, and an abundance of video recording devices, for it to have been a pre-meditated or planned murder.

Mere moments before Oscar Grant would be murdered by Johannes Mehserle, Anthony Pirone gave the order for Oscar to be arrested under Section 148 of the CA Penal Code, titled "Other Offenses Against Public Justice":

> Every person who willfully resists, delays, or obstructs any public officer, peace officer, or an emergency medical technician …
> in the discharge or attempt to discharge any duty of his or her office or employment, when no other punishment is prescribed, shall be punished by a fine not exceeding one thousand dollars ($1,000), or by imprisonment in a county jail not to exceed one year, or by both that fine and imprisonment.

The defense's "use of force" expert Greg Meyer testified that Grant was guilty of violating Section 148 by his "jumping" back onto the BART train once Pirone came upstairs and headed in his direction.

It must be noted that Pirone gave the order to arrest Oscar Grant *not* at the point that he removed

Grant from the train but *after* Oscar and his friends had protested Pirone's assault of Michael Greer, which was also after Pirone had twice assaulted Oscar Grant. When Pirone asked the train operator Keecha Williams if Grant or his friends were involved the "fight" she told him she did not know because she had not seen who was involved. The question of whether Oscar Grant should have even been arrested on the morning of Jan. 1, 2009, is a legitimate one.

Meyer would also later testify that Oscar Grant's standing up, after being told to sit on the platform, was also a violation of penal code 148 however, under cross examination by the prosecutor, it became obvious that Meyer's claim was flimsy:

Stein: Let's assume hypothetically Mr. Grant was directed -- escorted to the wall, told to have a seat, that's all he was told, and he sat down. And assume further that a couple of minutes later he stood up and at which point officer Pirone approached him and used an amount of physical force on him that resulted in him being forced back down to the ground. In that limited factual hypothetical, in your opinion he is arrestable for 148, Mr. Grant?

Meyer: Oh, that's - that's a mere - technically, yes, and and all by itself because in the hypothetical it's all by itself, that would be kind of a cheap arrest.

Stein posed the question to Meyer hypothetically however this is exactly what happened. Oscar Grant, Carlos Reyes, Jackie and Nigel Bryson obeyed the officers' instructions and sat on the Fruitvale platform against the wall. Once Pirone attacked their friend they rose to their feet but they did not leave the area where they had been directed to sit. Oscar Grant and his friends left their seated positions as a direct result of the criminal actions of Anthony Pirone.

After Pirone made the decision to arrest Grant, Oscar again rose to his feet to protest what he felt was an unfair arrest, inquiring "Who can we talk to?" He is forced back down on the platform by both Pirone and Johannes Mehserle who has now arrived on the scene. On his knees and speaking with Pirone (where Pirone utters the racial slur 'bitch ass nigga' twice) Oscar Grant voluntarily puts both his hands behind his back.

This begs the question, which we can word two ways: 1) why wasn't this good enough for Mehserle? Or, 2) why the *need* for Mehserle to decide the manner in which Oscar Grant would surrender and be placed under arrest?

Stein made the point that Mehserle and Pirone were working in tandem; Pirone's taunting of Grant in his face was the signal for Mehserle to abuse Grant physically. Pirone states defiantly "YEAH!" at the point that Oscar Grant is almost slammed down by Mehserle. The only possible 'need' to slam Grant down onto the platform would be to inflict punishment on him.

Once Oscar was on the ground, Pirone then quickly pinned Grant's head under his knee. Mehserle was behind Oscar Grant on top of his legs. Why, then, was it necessary to tase Grant if he was pinned down? If Oscar Grant's true intention was to produce a firearm to use against police (it wasn't), it would have been nonsensical – as well as suicidal – for him to wait until he was pinned down beneath two 200-plus-pound officers but that is beside the point. Oscar Grant, who had voluntarily complied with police orders, was now subdued beneath the knee of one officer with the other officer on top of his lower extremities: to deploy a taser on Oscar at this point would have simply been to inflict more punishment and pain. In short, it would have been to torture him.

Mehserle's own horribly rehearsed testimony shows that there was no need to deploy a taser against Oscar Grant since he was not resisting. Once again, I have quoted extensively from the trial transcript:

Stein: Tell me, when you got up off Mr. Grant and stepped back, what did you see?

Mehserle: My focus was just right on his back. I needed to pick where I needed to tase him. That's what I saw.

Stein: What about his hands? I thought that the hands were something you were concerned about? Could you see the hands at that time?

Mehserle: At the point that I made the decision to tase, my eyes went to his back and they never left his back.

Stein: Could you see his hands at that time?

Mehserle: No, sir.

Stein: And is that – do you know where his hands were at that time?

Mehserle:	The last time I saw his hands, his right hand was in his pocket. And then the next thing I saw, I focused on his back, sir.
Stein:	Were you in fear of your life – fear for your life at that time?
Mehserle:	I was afraid, yes, sir.
Stein:	Can you describe the level of – that you were afraid?
Mehserle:	Well, I didn't want to get shot.
Stein:	Did you think that you were very close to getting shot?
Mehserle:	I thought it was a possibility, yes, sir.
Stein:	And even at that time after believing that there's a possibility you're going to get shot, you never announced "gun, gun"; true?
Mehserle:	Correct.
Stein:	And you never said to officer Pirone or any of the other officers at that time "I think he's got a gun. I think he's got a gun"; true?
Mehserle:	I never said that.
Stein:	When you looked down and you were looking to see where you were going to shoot him with the probes … did Oscar Grant appear to be resisting you

in any way at that time?

Mehserle: At that time my focus was on his back. I had made the decision already to tase, so I don't – I don't specifically remember what Mr. Grant was doing, sir.

Stein: I'm sorry, you didn't see – you don't remember him –

Mehserle: At that point I don't remember what he was doing, sir.

Stein: Did you see anything consistent in your mind with resistance?

Mehserle: At the – at the point where I made the decision to tase, I fixed my eyes on where I needed to deploy the taser, where I needed to fire the taser, and that was – that was that. That was – that was – that's where my focus was.

Stein: And that's the point in time that I'm referring to. And at that point in time did you see anything that constituted resistance on the part of Mr. Grant?

Mehserle: The – the thought – the only thing that went through my head, the thought was that I needed to hurry up and tase. That's it. I didn't – there was no other thought. I didn't know if his – what his hands were doing. I didn't know where his feet were.

I didn't know any of that, sir.

Stein: Sir, I'm not asking what you were thinking at the time. I'm asking what you were you seeing. Do you remember seeing anything consistent with resistance?

Mehserle: No, sir.

The decision to deploy a 50,000 volt taser on a person who is laying prone, on their stomach, and not resisting must be called what it is: torture, plain and simple. The death of Oscar Grant was caused by the direct actions of both Pirone and Mehserle on the morning of Jan. 1, 2009. Their actions were acts of torture (actual and planned), as well as possibly mayhem; thus, both officers met the criteria for being charged with felony first degree murder.

It is not far-fetched to state that Mehserle should have been tried in this manner. When Alameda County Superior Court Judge Morris Jacobson made the decision to grant a change of venue to Johannes Mehserle's defense team on Oct. 16, 2009, Jacobson also stated his opinion on the case, saying that "Depending on the jury's attitude ... this could be anything from a first degree murder conviction to a complete acquittal."

Days before the start of Mehserle's trial a local government attorney stated he thought the initial decision to charge Mehserle with murder was correct. John Russo, currently the administrator for the City of Alameda and the former Oakland city attorney, stated that he "agree[d] with the DA's decision." Russo has not returned phone calls or e-mails to discuss this subject further.

Let's return for a moment to Orange County attorney Mark Cabaniss' analysis where he again expounds on the theory of First Degree Felony murder. Cabaniss applied his theory to the case of Kelly Thomas, a white 37-year old homeless schizophrenic who was beaten to death by 5-6 police officers in Fullerton, CA in July of 2011. Under "normal" circumstances Thomas would have been shielded from police murder through his white skin privilege and his familial law enforcement ties, but his social location and his disability meant that he had been "niggerized," to use the words of Cornel West; he was a castaway from white society and thus his life was expendable. Thomas' murderers were acquitted in January of 2014. Cabanniss' analysis, which could have easily been applied to Pirone and Mehsrle by the Alameda County District Attorney, puts forth a rationale for charging the police officers who attacked Thomas with felony first degree murder:

> ... the Orange County DA said ... that he had seen the unreleased surveillance tape, and had seen no evidence of intent to kill. Legally speaking, this is an inane non sequitur ... it simply has no legal significance to the case whatsoever. ... For example, kidnappers might accidentally leave their hostage locked up too long in an airtight room, where he suffocates. That would be felony murder, even if the kidnappers were racing home out of concern for their

hostage's air supply, and were delayed too long by a flat tire. The bottom line is simple, and for the defendant, brutal: In felony murder, intent is irrelevant.

So why is the DA talking about some legally meaningless point? A cynic might say that it looks like an attempt to mislead the public, telling them that there is not evidence of intent to kill, so that the public won't question a decision not to prosecute the police for murder. But the police can absolutely be prosecuted for murder even if Kelly Thomas' death was unintentional. I for one am betting that the DA knows this, since his office prosecutes felony murder cases all the time.

And I, for one, am betting that the Alameda County District Attorney's office also prosecutes felony murder cases all the time – they just aren't of cops who murder Black people.

I am also betting that Judge Robert Perry has presided over numerous felony first degree murder cases, but the case of People v. Johannes Mehserle would not be one of them:

Stein: ... with regard to the issues before the court this morning and as to whether or not this Motion should be granted, with regard to the first degree murder allegation, the court has heard all the evidence.

Judge Perry: I have.

Stein: And I'd ask the court to be mindful of the Penal Code section 189 which talks about premeditation and deliberation and that it need not take an extended period of time. So I think that when the court considers all the evidence, the court, I would ask, would determine that these are all factual determinations for the jury to make and I think that there is sufficient evidence that the court has heard, that this jury has heard, that these issues should go to the jury and the jury should make these calls.

... ...

Judge Perry: All right. I guess the issue, Mr. Stein, is that what did Bryson say, what is your recollection as to Bryson said Mehserle made some comment right before he fired, something to the effect of "screw this" or something? What is your recollection of that particular statement?

Stein: Well, with regard to that period of time, Mr. Bryson testified that repeatedly Grant said that he couldn't get his arm out. And after a period of time, Mr. Bryson testified that he heard the defendant say, "fuck this."

Judge Perry: I think that's what it was.

Stein: And at that point got up, pulled out his gun and fired it.

Judge Perry: See, I think probably that alone is enough to get this to the jury on a second degree murder charge, but let me make my ruling on that and then we're going to move on.

                …   …   …

Judge Perry: When I assess the evidence, as I must do in a light favorable to supporting the charge, I conclude the following: That the shooting occurred in a manner as to suggest an absence of premeditation and deliberation that is required for first degree murder. It's just clearly insufficient to support a first degree murder charge. … It will be up for the jury to make the decision and to assess the evidence, and I am going to allow a charge of second degree murder to go to the jury.

Under the system of white supremacy, police officers work for the state – the white supremacist state, be they white, black, brown, red or yellow. As it stands now, under the system of white supremacy in general, there is very little chance (infinitesimal) that any prosecutor will charge on-duty police officers with first degree murder in the deaths of Black people; that any judge will allow a first degree murder charge to remain on the table against a police officer who murdered a Black person in the United States;

and there is very little chance that any jury will find those police officers guilty of the first degree murder of a Black person.

Under the system of white supremacy in the specific case of People of the State of California v. Johannes Mehserle, there was very little chance that a white prosecutor would charge a white police officer with the first degree murder of a young Black man; that a white, pro-police judge would allow a first degree murder charge to stand against a white police officer who murdered a young Black man; and that a predominantly pro-police, "white-identified" jury would bring back a charge of murder – whether in the first or second degree - against that same officer.

The "fix" was in long before the actual crime of Oscar Grant's murder ever occurred. How that "fix" came about will be discussed in Chapter Six.

Tatiana Grant and her father, Oscar Juliuss, III. Photo courtesy of the Johnson Family.

Johannes Mehserle, murderer of Oscar Grant, is led into a Douglas County, Nevada courtroom on January 14, 2009. Photo courtesy of the San Francisco Bay View Newspaper.

Anthony Pirone, who shares culpability with Johannes Mehserle. Photo courtesy of the SF Bay View Newspaper.

Johannes Mehserle holding his taser. Photo taken by Oscar Grant on Jan. 1, 2009. Courtesy of Alameda County (CA) Superior Court.

Still photo from video taken by Tommy Cross on Jan. 1, 2009, of the murder of Oscar Grant by Johannes Mehserle at Fruitvale BART station. Carlos Reyes (1) yelling, "He's on my leg! He's on my leg!" as BART officer Tony Pirone (2) places his left knee on the head of Oscar Grant (3), and officer Johannes Mehserle (4) looks at and reaches for his automatic pistol. Also in this photo are BART officer Jonathan Guerra (5), Jackie Bryson (6) and Nigel Bryson (7). Photo courtesy of Alameda County Superior Court.

Michael Rains, defense attorney for Johannes Mehserle. Photo courtesy of Rains Lucia Stern, PC.

Judge Robert Perry also presided over the trial of Raphael Perez, former police officer at the center of the LAPD's notorious Rampart Scandal. Photo courtesy of the SF Bay View Newspaper.

Marisol Domenici. Photo courtesy of the SF Bay View Newspaper.

JR Valrey, Associate Editor of the San Francisco Bay View Newspaper, holds a flyer demanding "Justice for Oscar Grant"; to his left, "Chairman" Fred Hampton, Jr., son of slain Illinois Black Panther leader Fred Hampton, addresses crowd during pre-trial hearing of Johannes Mehserle, at Los Angeles County Superior Court. Author photo

"Justicia Para Oscar" - Justice for Oscar. Manila Ryce at pre-trial hearing for Johannes Mehserle at the Los Angeles County Superior Court Bldg. Author photo.

Center, left to right: Jack Bryson, father of Jackie and Nigel Bryson; Cephus Johnson, at microphone, and Kenneth Johnson, uncles of Oscar Grant, outside of Los Angeles County Superior Court. Author photo.

Min. Keith Muhammad escorts Wanda Johnson, mother of Oscar Grant, from the L.A. County Superior Court building. Photo courtesy of Charlene Muhammad.

"If You Want To Get Away With Murder Beome A Cop." Francisco Alvarez, protesting the sentence of Johannes Mehserle for Involuntary Manslaughter in the murder of Oscar Grant, at L.A. County Superior Court. Author photo

Tatiana and Oscar, by Miguel "Bounce" Perez

CHAPTER FIVE

If you want to get away with murder, become a cop

"… Dudley framed them because they were Negroes and had records and he knew there'd be no questions asked if they were killed resisting arrest."
~ 'Officer Edmund Exley' to 'Officer Bud White' in the 1997 film "L.A. Confidential"

Police murder of Black men in particular has been normalized to the point where it is reflected in Hollywood movies, as this quote from the Oscar–winning 1950s-period piece "L.A. Confidential" shows. The "blue wall of silence," which refers to the ways in which murder and other crimes by police are shielded from accountability and consequences, has also been normalized. Johannes Mehserle's murder of Oscar Grant follows the "playbook" for how this is done. The playbook of how these entities acted in concert with one another during Johannes Mehserle's murder trial has been mirrored elsewhere innumerable times. Using this trial as our lens (camera), the most basic, common elements are illuminated.

1. Slow response to investigate, charge and arrest the perpetrator

Johannes Mehserle was arrested for the murder of Oscar Grant almost two weeks after the incident.

While this length of time pales in comparison to cases such as George Zimmerman, the murderer of Trayvon Martin in Florida, there is one glaring fact that stands out: most murder investigations are just that – an attempt to find the person responsible for someone's death and bring them to account. In the case of Oscar Grant's murder, everyone knew who pulled the trigger.

California's own Governor "Jerry" Brown was even quoted as saying that, while he was "confident that [then-Alameda County District Attorney Tom Orloff was] carrying this investigation out in the manner he should," Brown was also said to have remarked that he didn't "understand why" it took two weeks for Orloff to make the decision to prosecute Johannes Mehserle.

The day of Oscar's funeral on Jan. 7, 2009, a protest march erupted into a rebellion in the streets of Oakland. This was also the day that Johannes Mehserle was scheduled to meet with BART internal investigators to discuss the shooting. According to Orloff, he made the decision to order Mehserle's arrest after Mehserle refused to at least make a statement to BART's investigators which could've shed some light on why he shot Grant. Orloff has not acknowledged the impact of the rebellion on his decision to arrest Mehserle but history has shown that only actions/mobilizations of critical mass (both violent *and* non-violent) have been able to secure concessions from the state for Black people and other

NO DOUBT: THE MURDER(S) OF OSCAR GRANT

peoples of color – even when those concessions are allegedly what the state says is its job in the first place: investigations and charging of crimes and arrests.

Cops are supposed to be held to a higher standard than the general public, yet when police blatantly violate that standard by breaking the law, District Attorneys are often loathe to prosecute them. One of the threats that is alleged to be hung over the heads of prosecutors is the implied refusal of cops to cooperate in future prosecutions due to a DA's punitive charging of a fellow officer. Such a threat speaks to the insanity of allowing police to police themselves.

One would think that since police officers live in the same society as 'law-abiding' and 'law-breaking residents,' it would seem that they should automatically possess the incentive to want to assist in the prevention, eradication and solving of crimes. For those officers who lack that incentive – the incentive to do the job we were told they were hired and sworn to do – they should be immediately replaced. Isn't that what happens to most of us when we don't do a job we've been hired to do?

2. Institutional protections are built-in from the beginning

Police are the protectors of the state and so, the state protects the police. Even when perpetrators tell the truth about their transgressions, the system is rigged to protect them. BART's Breath Alcohol Test (BAT) form is a case in point.

The institutional form that every officer must fill out when involved in a shooting automatically states that the shooting was an accident; there is an automatic belief in the officer's innocence. When a perpetrator such as Mehserle admits they have discharged their weapon intentionally, not by accident, the forms will not even allow for that – Mehserle had to handwrite a box on the form that said "discharge of weapon" and initial it. And, because of further institutional protection – this time in the form of the U.S. Constitution - the BAT form was not allowed into evidence to keep Mehserle from incriminating himself.

3. The perpetrator is not considered a threat to the Black public's safety

Approximately six weeks before murdering Oscar Grant, on Nov. 11, 2008, Johannes Mehserle and four other BART officers violently assaulted Kenneth Carrethers, an African American, for the latter's criticism of the BART police force after his car had been broken into at a train station parking lot. Carrethers stated that Mehserle and other officers "punched, kicked and eventually hog tied him," and that on the way to a hospital to treat his injuries Mehserle asked him, "Well, have you learned not to mess with police officers?" Mehserle said that

Carrethers had taken a "fighting stance" against him and he, along with the other officers, simply subdued him. Charges against Carrethers, who had been arrested for assaulting the BART officers, were dropped in late January, 2009, as Mehserle was seeking bail for the murder of Oscar Grant. A jury, with no Black folks on it (again), eventually cleared Mehserle and the other officers in Dec. of 2011 of excessive use of force, not that they didn't beat Carrethers up.

When an officer-involved shooting occurs, most departments take the officer out of the field and place them on either paid or non-paid leave. The officer may be assigned to desk duty while an investigation of the shooting is held, and some sort of assessment is made of the officer's state of mind. To my knowledge, no such type of intervention routinely occurs when an officer viciously assaults someone. No analysis is made of whether or not the officer is likely to engage in violent behavior again, and no interrogation of the racial dynamics or impact of the officer's violence is made when the victims of police assaults are people of color. The officer is usually allowed to remain "in the field" where they will continue to come into contact with – and be a potential threat to – other people of color.

Carrethers filed a lawsuit against the officers; that and the murder of Oscar Grant are the reasons we know about his case. To my knowledge Carrethers did not file a complaint with BART at the time he was assaulted, so there may not be any paperwork on that. Even if he had done so, however, it probably would not have been allowed into court during Mehserle's trial for Oscar Grant's murder. In California, the Peace Officer's Bill of Rights Act (POBRA), in conjunction with different parts of the state's penal code, has blocked regular folks from gaining access to the personnel files of police officers. Citing the officer's right to privacy, we are unable to know if an officer has a history of shootings and brutality complaints; we are also unable to find out if an officer has a record of domestic violence or other such acts while the officer is "off duty."

At the time of Oscar's murder, Mehserle had been on the BART police force just under four years. That is more than enough time to rack up multiple brutality complaints, however we are unable to know the truth of this thanks to POBRA.

In one slight detour from the playbook, the Alameda County Superior Court Judge who oversaw Mehserle's bail hearing, Morris Jacobson, stated that he did consider Mehserle to be a "danger to society … a flight risk with a character flaw," and that Mehserle was someone who had a "clear propensity for violence." Jacobson did not veer completely from the playbook however, since he did not remand Mehserle into custody and keep him behind bars for the duration of the trial. Jacobson allowed bail for Johannes Mehserle on Jan. 30, 2009 since bail is *guaranteed* by the U.S. and California constitutions –

the documents of "the people." Mehserle's bail was set at $3 million dollars, which Jacobson based on his assessment of Mehserle's character (or lack thereof) and the fact that he did not trust Mehserle to show up to trial due to inconsistencies in his statements and in his motion for bail. Mehserle was released approximately one week later when his bail was posted in part by the California Peace Officers Research Association and the California Police Officers Association.

4. Character Assassination One – the victim was not "squeaky clean"

Character assassination of the victims of police murder is one of the oldest moves in the playbook. At the time of Oscar Grant's murder he was 22-years old. Like many young African American men his age, Oscar had prior run-ins with the law. Grant's criminal past was first reported on by the media and then spread amply and widely by Mehserle supporters and supporters of law enforcement *before* Mehserle's criminal trial ever took place. Michael Rains even attempted to argue in a pre-trial hearing that Grant was "prone" to resisting arrest.

"The notion of the "Black male predator," journalist and author Jill Nelson writes, "is so historically rooted in the American consciousness that we have come to accept the brutalization and murder of citizens by the police as an acceptable method of law enforcement … This attitude, ingrained since slavery, is nurtured and manipulated by the police, who are quick to release the prior-arrest or medical records of their victims, as if   getting   a   speeding ticket, or jumping a   subway   turnstile, or being a graffiti   artist, or smoking marijuana, or being mentally ill, or serving time in prison for any reason whatsoever, somehow justified being killed by the police."

5.   Character Assassination Two – the victim is not a victim; the victim is actually an aggressor

On April 23, 2010, Michael Rains' submitted to the court a motion which consisted of a series of requests to either admit or deny certain evidence and testimony in court, and admonishments to witnesses and jurors. The very first request Rains made asked that the court "require the District Attorney and prosecution witnesses refer to Oscar Grant by name, rather than referring to him as "the victim" since, in Michael Rains' exact words, "there's no evidence that a crime occurred."

Approximately one year prior, on April 3, 2009, the BART authority's response to the wrongful death lawsuit filed by Oscar Grant's family, stated that officers Anthony Pirone and Marisol Domenici had been attacked by Oscar and that he had "… willfully, wrongfully, unlawfully made an assault upon defendants and would have beaten, bruised and ill-treated them if defendants had not immediately defended themselves." The "assaults" referred to in the document were Oscar Grant's fictitious attempt to knee Pirone in the groin and his fictitious grabbing of Domenici's arm. These lies had been utterly exposed during preliminary hearings in Alameda County and were not a major part of Mehserle's trial once it had been moved to Los Angeles, however their stench continued to linger in the air like sulphur.

Michael Rains painted Oscar as the instigator of a fight on the BART train on New Year's Day 2009. Members of the group Oscar was traveling with stated there was no fight but an "attempted" fight or scuffle – rough pushing and shoving – that some of them were involved in. One witness testified that Oscar Grant had been held in a headlock with a man named David Horowitch (Horowitch denied he had been in a fight with Oscar Grant; other witnesses could not identify who the person was who had been in the altercation with Horowitch).

6.   It's everybody's fault *except* the perpetrator's

Blame is placed everywhere except with the person who commits the murder. Supporters of Johannes Mehserle maintain that had Oscar Grant not been "fighting," "causing trouble," or "resisting arrest," he would be alive today; they also claim that were Grant not a thug he would be alive today. Oscar Grant's character was trampled upon in order to frame him as someone who would be reasonably expected to defy police and resist arrest.

Blame was also heavily shifted to BART's police agency and their allegedly faulty training, specifically on the use of tasers. And yet for some reason, as was noted during the trial by the prosecutor, Johannes Mehserle had never noticed or had an issue with his inadequate, BART-supplied training prior to murdering Oscar Grant. Under cross-examination, it was clear Mehserle either forgot or chose to ignore established BART protocols for dealing with persons suspected of having firearms on their persons.

In a July 4, 2010 letter released to the public as he awaited the jury's verdict, Johannes Mehserle stated that he never *intended* to shoot Oscar Grant. In his Nov. 4, 2010 statement to the court on the day of his sentencing Johannes Mehserle stated, "To the Grant family, to your Honor, and to the public at large, *I want you to know that the actions I took which led to Mr. Grant's death were based on Mr. Grant's actions* and his reaction to my *intent* to handcuff him …" [Emphasis mine]. Mehserle used the word *intentions* five times in his statement; the words *accidentally* and *mistake* three times; and the words *accident* and *unintentional* once. At no point whatsoever did Johannes Mehserle ever accept responsibility specifically for his unnecessary "need" to slam Oscar Grant into the platform's concrete floor in order to handcuff him, which is what led to Grant's death. Had *this* specific action not been taken by Mehserle, Oscar Grant probably would have made it home to his family that New Year's morning. Everything and anything, including the victims themselves, is/are usually blamed for the murder of people of color by law enforcement except the true culprit: white supremacy. White supremacy is the system that law enforcement agencies defend to the death (of people of color).

7. Automatic belief in the perpetrator's innocence and practical support are the tangible rewards of white privilege

Johannes Mehserle made no statements to the public or to BART investigators about what led to his shooting of Oscar Grant the morning of Jan. 1, 2009. Although by law, whatever he would have stated to BART investigators could not be used against him in *any* legal proceeding, instead of appearing at his Jan. 7, 2009 appointment to speak with BART authorities, Mehserle's then-attorney appeared stating his client had resigned from the agency. Mehserle then fled the state of California and went to Nevada, he claimed, due to threats against his life. Although he was considered a flight risk and a threat to public safety; he was nonetheless granted bail set by the court at $3 million dollars, an exorbitant amount that can only be explained in light of the nature of his crime and his having fled the jurisdiction.

Mehserle was not fired; he voluntarily resigned his position. Yet and still, he was able to enjoy the privilege of law enforcement support through 1) having his bail and his legal defense paid for by a non-profit association of law enforcement officers; 2) donations for family and legal support solicited by his *former* employer the BART police department, as well as various police association websites; 3) and his attorney Michael Rains actually requested in court that he should maintain the privilege and 'prestige' of the occupation he voluntarily resigned from by being referred to as 'Officer' Mehserle.

8.   Questionable conduct of fellow officers

Former Officer Tony Pirone stated that he clearly remembered Mehserle verbally state that he was going to tase Oscar Grant, but Pirone did not clearly remember that Oscar Grant was actively trying to physically assault him by kneeing him in the groin. Former Officer Marisol Domenici testified during preliminary hearings in Northern California that Oscar Grant had grabbed her arm and that she was in fear for her life and the lives of her fellow officers because the scene of the incident was so unruly and chaotic. Domenici even told BART's internal investigators that she felt so unsafe on the Fruitvale platform that she thought she would have to draw her own service weapon at some point. The video evidence and witness testimony by BART riders and BART's own surveillance camera (both in Northern California and later in the Los Angeles criminal trial) clearly showed that such was not the case.

Domenici's lies about the nature of the Fruitvale platform on Jan. 1, 2009, were so obviously bad that this writer was able to ascertain that Domenici had received some kind of coaching from legal counsel for her appearance in Los Angeles; Domenici's responses to the prosecutor's questions were not answers, but explanations of her previous answers in her Northern California testimony. Her performance on the witness stand was that bad.

Witnesses in most murder trials do not usually have contact with a defendant while the trial is going on; that is usually referred to as tampering. Curiously, Domenici's and Pirone's support of their fellow officer was evident not only in their lies on the witness stand but in their choice of wardrobe on the days they testified in Los Angeles. Domenici, Pirone and Mehserle were all dressed in light grey business suits; Pirone and Mehserle both had on yellow ties.

9. The Judge and the Jury are in on it, too

THE JUDGE in Johannes Mehserle's murder trial, Robert Perry, a former federal prosecutor, was assigned after Alameda County Superior Court Judge Morris Jacobson ruled that the trial should be moved to Los Angeles County on Oct. 17, 2009.

The Alameda County District Attorney's office charged Mehserle with murder but left the specific charge or degree open. At the end of the trial Judge

Perry promptly took the option of finding Mehserle guilty of First Degree Murder off the table. After the jury found Mehserle guilty of involuntary manslaughter and of intentionally using a gun, Perry dismissed the gun charge by saying he erred giving the jury the proper instructions on the gun allegation – even though he had utilized close to three hours to go over the instructions with the jury. The gun enhancement charge would have automatically added 10 years to Mehserle's sentence. By convicting Mehserle of the gun enhancement charge it appears the message the jury was attempting to send was that Mehserle had used a gun in the commission of a crime however, due to the error in the instructions, Judge Perry ruled that the finding of Involuntary Manslaughter (an "accident") was inconsistent with using a gun intentionally.

Additionally, after Perry stated the evidence in the trial did not show that Mehserle had *intended* to shoot Oscar Grant, he sent Mehserle off with a parting gift: he sentenced Mehserle to the lowest possible term: two years in state prison. Involuntary Manslaughter is classified as a "non violent" crime in the State of California; thus by law, all non violent offenders are given one day of credit for every day they serve behind bars. When factoring in Mehserle's jail time a) from his initial arrest in Nevada on January 14, 2009, till his b) February 6, 2009 release on bail, added to his c) being placed in custody immediately after the criminal trial ended on July 8, 2010, d) up to the day he was sentenced on November 5, 2010, Perry determined that Mehserle's actual time spent behind bars equaled 365 days, thereby satisfying the 2-year or 730-day sentence, and he was released from the Los Angeles County Men's Jail in the early morning hours of June 13, 2011. Although Perry stated in his remarks that Mehserle was sentenced to state prison, Mehserle never left the jurisdiction of the Los Angeles County Jail system.

Calling Mehserle's sentence a "parting gift" is quite apt. Journalist Lance Williams wrote that Perry gave Mehserle a "big break" when he sentenced him to the low end term of 2-years for Oscar's murder. Quoting from the report "Time Served on Prison Sentence" published by California's Department of Corrections in March, 2010, Williams stated "The data shows that Californians who haven't killed anybody routinely do more prison time than the sentence Mehserle [received]. People convicted of armed robbery served 54.5 months – more than double Mehserle's term. People convicted of selling controlled substances served 33 months. Californians who spent 24 months in state prison – Mehserle's sentence – had been convicted of such crimes as assault and battery, escape, or possession of controlled substances for sale."

According to Williams, the data in the report "...doesn't distinguish between those convicted of involuntary manslaughter, as was Mehserle, and the more serious crime of voluntary manslaughter," therefore, we are unable to compare Mehserle's sentence to all others sentenced for Involuntary Manslaughter in the State of California. We can however, say with certainty that, on average, Mehserle served less time than those imprisoned for kidnapping, rape, vehicular manslaughter, assault with a deadly weapon, arson, plain old assault, and *all* felonies in the State of California.

We can also say with certainty that Mehserle served less time in jail than Michael Vick did for his involvement in running a dog fighting ring (sentenced to 23 months; served approximately 20 months), and Plaxico Burress did for shooting himself (sentenced to 24 months; served approximately 21 months).

Judge Perry is known to anti-police brutality activists in Los Angeles as being a "friend" to cops due to what they consider to be the lenient sentencing given to Rafael Perez. Perez is the former LAPD officer at the center of the notorious "Rampart Scandal." Perry sentenced Perez to five years in state prison on a charge of theft (stealing cocaine from the evidence room). The trade off was that Perez cooperated with prosecutors in providing information on himself, his partner and several other officers on the beatings and shootings of several Angelenos, along with the planting of evidence on their persons. To say that the "Rampart Scandal" "rocked" the City of Los Angeles is an understatement. And if that wasn't enough, it was Perry who ordered Perez's release from a local detention facility – not a state prison where he had been sentenced (similar to Mehserle) after three years and allowed him to serve his parole outside of the state of California.

Former Los Angeles prosecutor Vincent Bugliosi, responsible for convicting the Charles Manson family and a best-selling author, believes that the general public should have more skepticism and less veneration when it comes to court judges. "The American people," he writes, "Have an understandably negative view of politicians, public opinion polls show, and an equally negative view of lawyers. Conventional logic would seem to dictate that since a judge is normally both a politician and a lawyer, people would have an opinion of them lower than a grasshopper's belly. But on the contrary, the mere investiture of a twenty-five dollar Black cotton robe elevates the denigrated lawyer-politician to a position of considerable honor and respect in our society as if the garment itself miraculously imbues the person with qualities not previously possessed."

THE JURORS in Johannes Mehserle's trial were drawn from a pool of over 100 potential Angelenos who were all given a questionnaire. I must note however, that not all 100 of the potential jurors went through the process of voir dire; Judge Perry felt that a representative group had been chosen while approximately 20-30 potential jurors remained who had filled out questionnaires.

According to Bay Area television station KGO legal analyst Dean Johnson, a practicing Northern

California attorney and a widely-known authority on criminal law in California, Judge Morris Jacobson was reported to have "… warned the defense that even though this case is going out of Alameda County, [that] is not an excuse to be discriminatory in the selection of jurors and in particular the judge said, "You are not going to exclude African American jurors from this jury wherever the case is tried." But that is exactly what happened. Not a single person of direct African descent was picked to sit on the trial of Johannes Mehserle for the murder of Oscar Grant. This writer personally viewed the juror selection process and noted that, after Rains' initial courtroom antics to have law enforcement officers sit on the jury (they are barred from doing so by California law), both the prosecution and the defense struck African Americans from the jury pool through the use of "peremptory strikes" – the process whereby both sides can dismiss jurors for whatever reason or 'non' reason they like.

Michael Rains' motion for a change of venue had notoriously labeled African Americans as being incapable of reasonably sifting through the evidence and finding his client anything but guilty. His motion was inflammatory in that Rains stated a *separate* voir dire process would have to be undertaken with each prospective African American juror in order to determine if they could truly be non-biased. So determined was he to keep Blacks off the jury, that this writer personally watched him peremptorily strike two African American jurors who had *significant* ties to law enforcement; one, a Black man whose wife was a 20-plus-year employee of the Los Angeles Police Department; the other, a Black woman whose sister was a Los Angeles County Sheriff.

In her work *The New Jim Crow*, Michelle Alexander writes that

> "… the Supreme Court and lower courts have tolerated all but the most egregious example of racial bias in jury selection, and this is usually put in practice through something called "peremptory strikes" … What this means in practice is that peremptory strikes are notoriously discriminatory. In addition, jury pools tend to be disproportionately white for a number of reasons, including the felony-disenfranchisement laws that permanently exclude 30% of men from jury service for life."

No effort was made whatsoever on the part of the prosecutor or the judge to say "Hold up, wait a minute, let's get a couple of Black folks on this jury." A Batson motion to challenge the exclusion of Black jurors could have been filed by the District Attorney but was not. In Batson v. Kentucky, a case involving a Black man accused of burglary and an all-white jury that convicted him, the Supreme Court held that prosecutors could not peremptorily strike all Black jurors from cases with Black defendants without showing good cause. The Supreme Court also held that "… By denying a person participation in jury service on account of his race, the State also unconstitutionally discriminates against the excluded juror. Moreover, selection procedures that purposefully exclude Black persons from juries undermine public confidence in the fairness of our system of justice."

You can say that again.

"Moreover, selection procedures that purposefully exclude Black persons from juries undermine public confidence in the fairness of our system of justice."

The questionnaire for all of the prospective jurors asked a wide variety of things ranging from their backgrounds to their relationships with law enforcement to whether or not they were familiar with Oakland's crime rate, and if they believed that police officers lie. Although Oscar Grant's murder took place in Oakland, he was born and raised in Hayward, about 20 miles or so south of the city. Asking potential Los Angeles jurors if they are familiar with the crime rate of a city more than 350 miles away should be seen as damning and prejudicial, but that is not the worst part. If ever there was evidence needed for a charge of rigging a trial this one question to the potential jurors – 'do police officers lie' – that both the defense and the prosecution allowed into the questionnaire should win the prize.

Of course police officers lie. That is a matter of fact, not hatred, conjecture, or fantasy but fact. Police officers lie so much and so often after taking an oath to tell the truth on witness stands across the country that Sarah Burns even makes mention of it in her book on the Central Park Five. Burns notes that the practice has a nickname: Testilying.

I can only wonder how many of the potential jurors in this trial who answered yes to the question 'do police officers lie?' were summarily dismissed.

Mehserle's jurors were more than likely not privy to the transcripts of his preliminary hearing in Oakland except when excerpts of witness testimony were referred to by Rains or the prosecutor. All prospective jurors are almost routinely asked if they can render a verdict based solely on the evidence presented before them in court. Those jurors who make it past voir dire to serve are then reminded – and admonished – that their decision can only be made based on the evidence that is put before them in court. And yet, the extent to which jurors who live in a white supremacist state bring preconceived notions with them into a court room has not been acknowledged or discussed thoroughly enough, in my opinion.

The jury in this case has been described at times as being "all white." Based simply on observation this writer personally witnessed one juror (originally an alternate) of Asian descent, and at least four jurors (male and female) who were Latino. But the classification of Latino is a rather thorny issue that cannot be sorted out in this book. Suffice to say that how a person classifies themselves can be (and in many instances, actually is) different from how census forms classify them, which may be different from how neighbors, persons on the street and journalists sitting across from them may classify them.

Be that as it may, based on their answers to questions posed by the prosecutor, of the 12 predominantly White/Latino jurors initially picked for this trial, five had family or friends who were law enforcement or did business with law enforcement; of the 6 original alternates, two had family or friends who were law enforcement or, these individuals wanted to pursue law enforcement as a career.

The sixth amendment to the United States Constitution states that a defendant has a right to an impartial jury; there is no mandate in the Constitution, there is no "right," that a defendant has to be tried by "a jury of his or her peers." On the contrary, the Constitution does state that jurors must be chosen from a cross-section that represents "the community." The jurors in the murder trial of Johannes Mehserle neither represented a cross-section of the community where Oscar Grant was murdered (Alameda County), nor where the trial of his murderer was held (Los Angeles County).

Once the jury was chosen they were ordered semi-sequestered by Judge Perry in an effort to shield them from any influences other than the testimony in court. Jurors were not held in an undisclosed location, locked away from family and friends; they were simply gathered together in location for pick-up and drop-off from court so as not to view protestors outside of the courthouse. Despite the significance of this trial and its implications the jurors, sadly, opted not to speak with the media once they were released from jury service. Although it was each juror's absolute right to exercise this decision, a wonderful opportunity to shed light on their thinking process and the dialogues that took place during deliberations, as well as an accounting for their actions, was "kicked to the curb" since the jurors chose to remain silent and anonymous. Silence and anonymity are also some of the spoils of white supremacy.

10. A brief word on prosecutors

The words 'prosecute' and 'persecute' come from the same Latin root – to follow or pursue. Those who have historically 'pursued' people of Afrikan descent cannot be expected to whole-heartedly advocate for justice on their behalf. Prosecutors routinely over charge Black people who are suspected of crimes, while routinely under charging whites who are suspected of crimes against Black people. Additionally, there is the working relationship that prosecutors enjoy with police officers; in the cases of police murder of Black people, this relationship is usually described as Frank James investigating Jesse

James. In Mehserle's case, I would grade the prosecutor who actually tried the case (an assistant district attorney) with a C-minus for less than vigorous courtroom delivery. Although the prosecution's trial brief laid out his theory of the case that I basically agreed with – that Mehserle (and Anthony Pirone) were unnecessarily brutal towards Oscar Grant and that Mehserle intentionally drew his weapon – Mehserle should have had someone sitting next to him in Los Angeles and they both should have been charged with Felony First Degree Murder.

11. The media works for the cops, not the public

Media outlets routinely parrot the words of government officials and the police. Some outlets defend this practice as necessary because, should they fail to do so, they believe (or have been told) they will be cut off from "crucial" and "valuable" access to information. Sometimes the media will go beyond parroting or cheer-leading. In Johannes Mehserle's case, the media conveniently handed him his defense against murder before his defense even came up with a defense.

Five days after Grant's murder, on Jan. 6, 2009, the *San Francisco Chronicle's* Demian Bulwa reported that Johannes Mehserle still had not made any statements to BART investigators or the press (through his attorney) of how the incident occurred. This may also have been the genesis of Mehserle's

"Taser defense" in the media:

> While BART has said little
> publicly, a source familiar with the
> investigation said the agency is
> looking into many leads, including
> the possibility that the officer had
> intended to fire his Taser stun gun
> instead of his gun. Don Cameron,
> a former BART police sergeant and
> weapons expert who now teaches
> police officers about proper use of
> force, said Monday that he had
> watched footage of Grant's death
> and was convinced that the officer
> had meant to fire a Taser - a
> device that he said BART began
> using recently.

The *San Francisco Chronicle* handed this convenient
legal defense to Johannes Mehserle courtesy of
someone intimately linked to his then-employer, the
Bay Area Rapid Transit Authority. It was, I guess, to
be expected that the *Chronicle* would have as their go-
to-expert a former BART police officer. This
particular officer's background should give us pause:
as a use of force expert and trainer of law
enforcement personnel, Cameron regularly testifies
on behalf of police who find themselves on "the
other side of the table" in a courtroom. Cameron was

originally slated to be a witness for Mehserle's defense but was not called to testify in the Los Angeles criminal trial. An article in the *San Francisco Weekly* described Cameron's job of offering expert testimony as rationalizing "… what victims describe as vicious beatings into benign-seeming narratives about officers who merely followed police protocols and court-defined standards of reasonable force. In some of these cases, Cameron seems to explain away behavior that is in no way gentle."

Prior to handing Mehserle his defense, the media placed the blame solely on his gun. One of the first news reports on the Fruitvale shooting, appearing New Year's morning 2009 around 11:39 a.m. on the *Oakland Tribune's* website stated "… an officer's gun discharged, wounding Grant …", as if the gun had no help in the pulling of its trigger. The officer's identity was conveniently shielded by the *Tribune*.

12. The 'soul murder' of the victim's community continues through callous disregard

Oscar Grant had been assaulted three times, cursed at and called a racial slur on the morning of his murder in less than 15 minutes. As can be seen on the videos taken by BART train riders, he is on his knees several seconds before Mehserle murders him, seemingly pleading with Officer Tony Pirone not to physically harm him. His head and neck would soon be pinned under the knee of the 200-plus pound officer. Jackie Bryson, kneeling next to Oscar Grant, said Oscar told Pirone he could not breathe. After Johannes Mehserle shot Oscar Grant in the back, he handcuffed Grant and searched him for weapons, kneeling on his back not far from where the blood was oozing out   .

In the Los Angeles trial there were numerous photos and documents entered into evidence and labeled in chronological order. During one afternoon session, Michael Rains referred to a defense exhibit that had not been entered into evidence.   He apologized to the court for his oversight and was allowed to continue. When asked to label the document in question – a diagram of a body meant to represent Oscar Grant at autopsy – Rains said to label the Exhibit "KKK." The representation of a black body murdered by a white police officer, labeled with the initials of an organization whose history is drenched in the blood of murdered black bodies, was duly noted by most of the African-American observers in attendance at the trial.

Sometimes, the soul murder was unintentional, but it happened nonetheless. During that same afternoon session, Dr. Thomas Rogers, the pathologist who performed the autopsy on Oscar Grant, testified that there was evidence of blunt force trauma to Oscar's head. Rogers said he could not pinpoint the exact time the wound occurred but speculation in the courtroom amongst some observers, as well as journalists, was that Tony

Pirone's assault of Oscar Grant had caused the wound. Wanda Johnson, Oscar's mother, began to weep as Rogers testified; she was barely audible.

Rogers: … when I peeled back the scalp in order to expose the skull, and there was an area of hemorrhage that was basically on the left side of the head above the ear, measured about half an inch in greatest dimension. And to me, this is consistent with some form of blunt force trauma.

Stein: When you use that term blunt force trauma as a pathologist, you've seen some kind of blow to the side of the head?

Rogers: Well, a blow is one possibility. There are an infinite number of different types of blunt force trauma. What you just said is one possibility.

Stein: For the record, what kind of other types of blunt force trauma might you be looking at?

Rogers: Well, for instance, instead of a blow to the head, if somebody falls down and hits their head, this could cause the same thing.

Stein: All right. So this area of hemorrhage could be from a blow, it could be from a kick, or it could be from falling down?

Rogers: Or – That's correct, or an infinite number of other different things.

Stein: From your observation of this particular hemorrhage, were you able to determine, sir, whether or not the hemorrhage may have occurred shortly before death or within days of death?

Rogers: Not totally. And by that I mean – first of all, the fact that hemorrhage was there, that means whatever caused it caused it while the individual was living.

Judge Perry: All right. Let's take a break, ladies and gentlemen. I'll put you in the back for a moment.

Wanda Johnson's sobbing was more than audible now. Judge Perry declaring of a brief recess and clearing the courtroom was so that Johnson's crying would not unduly prejudice the jury *against* Mehserle.

An echo chamber was created that slandered Oscar Grant, as well as his friends and his family throughout this entire ordeal. The slander of Oscar Grant had its genesis in legal arguments in the press and in the courtroom. Both Oscar and his friends were said to be responsible for Oscar's death. The forces of white supremacy operating through law enforcement were essentially blameless. This echo chamber contained some of the most vile and vulgar commentary imaginable, including 1) Oscar got what he deserved, 2) Oscar's daughter Tatiana was better off being fatherless and 3) Oscar's family was simply looking for a multi-million dollar settlement all along.

The 'soul murder' continued during the sentencing of Johannes Mehserle for Oscar Grant's murder. Michael Rains argued that his client was suitable for probation, not imprisonment, since Mehserle did not have a (documented) history of violence, and had received a favorable psychological evaluation from a court appointed psychologist. Rains stated there was precedent for his client to receive probation and that precedent was the case of liquor store owner Soon Ja Du.

Du was convicted of voluntary manslaughter on November 15, 1991, in the murder of 15-year old Latasha Harlins. Du grabbed Harlins, accusing her of attempting to steal a $2 bottle of orange juice from her store. Harlins hit Du in an effort to break Du's grip; Du pulled a handgun from behind the counter and shot Harlins in the back of the head as the teenager was walking away from her. Du's conviction carried a maximum possible sentence of 16 years in state prison but the judge in that case sentenced Du to five years of probation, four hundred hours of community service, and a $500 fine.

For Michael Rains to set foot in a Los Angeles courtroom and argue that his murdering client should receive probation for the death of Oscar Grant because some other murderer – the murderer of Latasha Harlins – was given probation left this writer with no words at the time.

Since that time, I have found and relied on the words of the late psychologist Dr. Bobby E. Wright of Chicago. Dr. Wright labeled this type of behavior exhibited by white supremacists as psychopathic.

Indeed.

CHAPTER SIX

The Genesis

Johannes Mehserle committed the act that caused Oscar Grant's murder on scores of video recordings. The video footage shows, amongst other things, Mehserle with what appears to be a surprised look on his face after he shoots Oscar in the back; at another point in the videos Mehserle is seen putting both hands to his head, almost as if to say "What just happened?" In order to better understand "what just happened" at the Fruitvale station in the early morning hours of Jan. 1, 2009, it is necessary to have an accurate understanding of white supremacy.

Charles Mills, Northwestern University philosophy professor and author of *The Racial Contract*, defines global white supremacy as, "… a political system, a particular power structure of formal or informal rule, socioeconomic privilege, and norms for the differential distribution of material wealth and opportunities, benefits and burdens, rights and duties."

Mills gives us a good starting point. We must, however, add two more key points: the "public and psychological wage" that Dr. W.E.B. DuBois, sociologist, scholar, activist and co-founder of the National Association for the Advancement of Colored People (NAACP), spoke of in his 1935 book *Black Reconstruction in America: 1860-1880*; and the concept of *violence*.

DuBois' life spanned the years from 1868 until 1963, and as a trained sociologist he observed society from a vantage point far different and far vast than the average person. According to DuBois, the "public and psychological wage" consists of the non-economic *yet still tangible* benefits that working class whites receive from the ruling class whites who exploit them: the planters, the land and factory-owning industrialists, bankers and directors/owners of corporations (multi- national or not). These wages can be considered a form of unearned, "cultural currency."

As a global political system, the program of white supremacy has historically been carried out and continually reproduces itself through coercion and physical force. In her work *Killing Rage Ending Racism*, cultural critic and feminist theorist bell hooks says that, "it is important that everyone in the United States understand that white supremacy promotes, encourages, and condones all manner of violence against black people. [White supremacy] allows this violence to remain unseen and/or renders it insignificant by suggesting it is justifiable punishment for some offense."

Mills labels the military, the penal system and the police as "the coercive arms of the state." Kristian Williams writes that, " … the police represent the most direct means by which the state imposes its will on the citizenry … when the persuasion, indoctrination, moral pressure, and incentive measures all fail there are the police."

Interestingly enough, DuBois wrote that "the police were drawn from" the ranks of the white working class.

Paraphrasing bell hooks, both whites and Blacks in the U.S. have been deliberately socialized to think that white supremacy is personal prejudice by one individual against another individual or a group of people based on their skin color. NO. White supremacy is, according to hooks, " … a consciously mapped out strategy of domination that [is] systematically maintained."

In plainer words: White supremacy is societal policy that is heavily dependent on psychological acceptance by and psychological favors rendered to white folks (persons of European/Caucasian descent or who are marked as white); it is maintained by violence and the police are the main purveyors of this violence; historically, the ranks of the police forces in this country have been comprised primarily of those working class white folks who have been the targets of the psychological conditioning of and the recipients of the psychological favors of "whiteness."

Because white supremacy is an institution it reproduces itself and outlasts individuals; its "consciously mapped out strategy of domination" can be carried out unconsciously by not just whites but by Black people and other people of color also. "The racial divide was initiated in a period of very explicit and intentional racism, but has continued through to our present situation where explicit intention is not necessary to turn out the same disparities," says Rinku Sen, the executive director of the Applied Research Center (ARC), a racial justice 'think-research-work' tank. "Contemporary structural racism (white supremacy) is a system in which you have racism without racists. So, when you are building systems atop racist structures, even if you have no intention to create racial divides, or you don't feel any racial animus yourself, the system starts to perpetuate

169

racism anyway. Intention is not required in order to produce racist impact."

The global system of white supremacy governs our everyday lives here in the U.S. and permeates every area of our existence, across various disciplines (law, education, medicine, literature, art, aesthetics, philosophy, politics, sports, etc.). At the heart of this institution are beliefs about whiteness. Phyllis Jackson, Associate Professor of Art History and former member of the Black Panther Party, identifies these beliefs about whiteness as "The 5 Promises" which comprise the areas of Intelligence, Aesthetics, Morality, Sexuality and Culture. Under white supremacy, whites believe they are superior to everyone because they (whites) 1) are the most intelligent; 2) are the most beautiful; 3) possess the most appropriate moral character; 4) possess the most appropriate sexual nature and 5) come from the most appropriate cultural background.

"These promises tell you instantly how they are going to treat someone who they do not identify as white," says Jackson. The result: persons who are not white will never, ever "measure up." They will forever be seen as "less than." Whiteness epitomizes humanity; the less white you are, the less "human" you are.

Khalil Gibran Muhammad notes as much in his work, *The Condemnation of Blackness: Race, Crime, and the Making of Modern Urban America,* when he links how Black culture became "incriminated" while European immigrants' culture was "humanized" as the U.S. entered the 20th century. This is crucial to philosophically understanding how white supremacy works. It explains the thoughts of Immanuel Kant, regarded as one of the Western world's greatest philosophers. Kant was actually an anthropology teacher however, when you consider that the social concept of race is scientifically sanctioned, it makes sense. Kant, who lived from 1724 until 1804, could say in a comment on the words of a Black man who was speaking to someone else, "... it might be that there were something in this which perhaps deserved to be considered; but in short, this fellow was quite black from head to foot, a clear proof that what he said was stupid."

Kant completely discounted what came out of the man's mouth simply because the man was Black. The same discounting takes on a new turn in today's society: instead of taking away, stuff gets piled on because the person is not white: "Of course he or she is a thug, a criminal, a scumbag, a gang member, a drug dealer, on welfare, a prostitute: he or she is Black."

This European worldview is how the deck had been stacked for Johannes Mehserle and against Oscar Grant long before both young men were ever born. The American worldview that rigged the system for Johannes Mehserle and against Oscar Grant began with the founding of this country on stolen land, with stolen people, and built with stolen labor.

An agreement was made at the founding of the U.S. between its rulers and its citizens known as the social contract. This contract gives the government the consent of the citizenry to rule over them; it is where the government – the state – gets its authority and its legitimacy to govern and the U.S. Constitution is the formal evidence of the contract. Human rights scholar and author Dr. Y. N. Kly writes that "when the U.S. Constitution was written, more than 50% of the population over which it was to eventually serve as the basis for legitimate government was non-Anglo-American and non-European, and thus nonparticipant in its formation." Kly argues that "through constitutional omission by not having the Africans and Native Americans represented in the formulation of the Constitution," this act created at the same time an anti-social contract that, while not legitimate, is the informal agreement for how the state rules over Africans, Native Americans and their descendants. It is also how landless and poor whites are ruled over which is why the "psychological wage" of white supremacy is so important: the "psychological wage" gives this class of whites "buy in" - a footing into a society that they will gladly defend but exploits them nonetheless. Mills puts it this way: "this 'Racial Contract,' is not a contract between everybody ('we the people'), but between just the people who count, the people who really are people ('we the white people')."

It is as if there are pieces of paper, with the Constitution, the Declaration of Independence and the Bill of Rights written on one side and on the other side, written in invisible ink, is the Racial Contract which renders people of Afrikan descent in particular as 'sub-persons' who must be kept in check at all times. These two classes (persons and those who are not) were recognized, coded, and enshrined in the United States' founding document.

It is for this reason Chief Justice Roger B. Taney could write in the Supreme Court's majority opinion in Dred Scott v. Sanford (1856) that:

"The words "people of the United States" and "citizens" are synonymous terms, and mean the same thing. They both describe the political body who, according to our republican institutions, form the sovereignty and who hold the power and conduct the Government through their representatives. They are what we familiarly call the "sovereign people," and every citizen is one of this people, and a constituent member of this sovereignty.

The question before us is whether the class of persons described in the plea in abatement [Afrikans] compose a portion of this people, and are constituent members of this sovereignty? We think they are not, and that they are not included, and were not intended to be included, under the word "citizens" in the Constitution, and can therefore claim none of the rights and privileges which that instrument provides for and secures to citizens of the United States."

Taney continued:

"On the contrary, they were at that time considered as a subordinate and inferior class of beings who had been subjugated by the dominant race, and, *whether emancipated or not*, yet remained subject to their authority, and had no rights or privileges but such as those who held the power and the Government might choose to grant them." [Emphasis mine].

In writing the Supreme Court's opinion Taney goes on to quote the language used in the Declaration of Independence, which he calls "equally conclusive:"

"The general words ... would seem to embrace the whole human family ... But it is too clear for dispute that the enslaved African race were not intended to be included, and formed no part of the people who framed and adopted this declaration ... the men who framed this declaration ... perfectly understood the meaning of the language they used, and how it would be understood by others, and they knew that it would not in any part of the civilized world be supposed to embrace the [Afrikan] race, which, by common consent, had been excluded from civilized Governments and the family of nations

… They spoke and acted according to the then established doctrines and principles, and in the ordinary language of the day, and no one misunderstood them."

It is for this reason Taney wrote Black people "had no rights which the white man was bound to respect …".

The process of humanizing one group of persons and de-humanizing another occurred simultaneously. This philosophy has remained, more or less intact, from that moment through today. This is the philosophical underpinning that lives and breathes side by side with the 14th Amendment to the United States Constitution which made Afrikan people and their descendants U.S. citizens. Afrikan people, Blacks, were omitted as full, consenting participants in the founding of this nation because they were considered not to be human … but they were considered to be property – private property.

UC Riverside Professor of Ethnic Studies Andrea Smith, a co-founder of Incite! Women of Color Against Violence, theorizes that "the logic of slavery" is one of several pillars that currently upholds white supremacy. According to this "logic," Blackness is equated with "slaveability" and "renders Black people as inherently 'slaveable' – nothing more than property."

Smith posits that prior to the Civil War the

majority of the South's prisoners were white but Black people became "re-enslaved" after the ratification of the 13th Amendment to the U.S. Constitution. Passed and ratified by the U.S. Congress in 1865, the 13th Amendment abolished slavery "except as a punishment for crime whereof the party shall have been duly convicted."

Through imprisonment and the convict-lease system, Smith says that Black people went from being the property of individual whites to the property of the state, thereby illustrating "the criminalization of Blackness as a logical extension of Blackness as property."

Former political prisoner and prison abolitionist Angela Davis notes that the 'Black Codes' (which were the revised version of the 'Slave Codes,' the legal/social guidelines for dealing with slaves) that were enacted after the Civil War covered many areas "that were criminalized only when the person charged was black." Quoting the great abolitionist Frederick Douglass, Davis writes that the Southern U.S. had a "tendency to impute crime to color."

The imputing of crime to color continues with what we know to be racial profiling. Within the logic of white supremacy Blackness equals criminal. Blackness equals guilt. In the words of noted legal scholar Derrick Bell, "By virtue of color alone, Blacks are suspect ..."

Thus saith the logic of white supremacy: "Of course what he said was stupid; he's Black. Of course she or he is dangerous, violent, a criminal, a thug, a gang member, a scumbag, a drug dealer, on welfare, a prostitute: she or he is Black."

This is the background that must be taken into consideration in order to better understand the murder(s) of Oscar Grant and all the others.

AFTERWORD

Black Lives Matter

Oscar Grant's life was taken unjustly. He was violently and unnecessarily ripped from his family and friends, his immediate community and from all of us by the callous and reckless yet deliberate actions of white supremacy. It is for these reasons and not because of convoluted legal language or the pronouncements of strangers that we call his death a murder. That's our story and we're sticking to it.

Oscar was no saint; this is true. But since when has being a saint *ever* been the prerequisite for the right to life? Never, except for those who are murdered by white supremacy. No other system denigrates Afrikan people as being sub-human while we are alive and then, after it murders us, demands that we should have been Uber human because we dared breathe air.

The audacity of us.

Oscar Grant had a right to life and his life had meaning to many but let us be crystal clear: Oscar Grant was not murdered because he was Oscar Juliuss, III, son of Oscar Julluss, Jr., or because he was Wanda Johnson's baby boy; Oscar Grant was not murdered because he was Sophina's fiance' or Tatiana's father. Oscar Grant was murdered because he was wearing the right uniform on Jan. 1, 2009. According to the logic of white supremacy he did not represent the home team: he represented the Other.

The murder of Oscar Grant on New Year's Day 2009 was not an isolated incident; it was both 1) part of a disturbing rash of anti-Black violence following the election of Barack Obama as the 1st African-American and 44th President overall of the U.S.; and 2) a long tradition of state violence – physical, coercive and deadly force committed by and on behalf of a government through its enforcers – the police – against Afrikan-descendant people.

Oscar Grant, Adolph Grimes and Robbie Tolan were all attacked by police within the 24-hour window of Dec. 31, 2008 - Jan. 1, 2009. Grimes was shot 14 times by police – 12 of the bullets hit him in the back – outside of his home in New Orleans, LA, and Tolan, son of former Major League baseball player Bobbie Tolan, was shot in the chest by a police officer who assumed Tolan had stolen his own car parked in his parents driveway in an affluent Texas suburb.

Violence committed by the state is considered legitimate because of the social contract between government and its citizens - The People. As a white supremacist state ("we the white people") the U.S. has a history of allowing coercive, deadly physical force to be used against enslaved and free Afrikans and their descendants. This coercive, deadly physical force is not only carried out and allowed by police but also by white individuals (vigilantes, self-appointed law enforcers, neighborhood watch captains), organizations and private security as well. This is how state violence is supposed to function since, in the words of UCLA Professor of History Robin D.G. Kelley, we live under a system that is "… designed to protect white privilege, property and personhood, and render black and brown people [as] predators, criminals, illegals, and terrorists …".

One of the ways violence by police is legitimated is by the repetition of their narrative which relieves them of accountability: "police have a dangerous job." That's their story and they're sticking to it. The truth however is far different.

Federal Bureau of Investigation (FBI) statistics track the numbers of police officers killed in the line of duty, killed accidentally, and both police and federal officers who are assaulted. The FBI also includes police officers in Puerto Rico who were killed.

According to the FBI a total of 48 police officers were killed in the line of duty nationwide in 2009, the year Oscar Grant was murdered, and:

2010	2011	2012
56	72	48

(the last year stats were available)

The Officer Down Memorial Page, a non-profit website dedicated to honoring fallen officers, lists all officer deaths as in the line of duty, whether accidental or not. The site also lists police dogs that have died (those numbers are a non-factor here):

2009	2010	2011	2012	2013
129	173	165	105	90

The numbers of people murdered by police nationwide, whether through direct execution such as Ramarley Graham in New York or Kenneth Harding in San Francisco, or through callousness and negligence such as Rekia Boyd in Chicago, is much, much harder to come by. One reason for this is because no one entity, governmental or private, has taken up this work.

The website for the Stolen Lives Project (www.stolenlives.org), which was a book created in 1999 to honor all of the victims of police murder and is a project of the October 22nd Coalition to Stop Police Brutality, Repression, and the Criminalization of a Generation, has not been updated since 2007.

Wikipedia maintains a "List of killings by law enforcement officers in the United States," but Wikipedia has never been known as a bastion of accuracy. Besides, Wikipedia admits that "The list … is incomplete, as the annual average number of justifiable homicides committed by law enforcement alone is estimated to be near 400." Wikipedia's listing is as follows:

2009	2010	2011	2012	2013
60	80	159	587	304

As of 2012 Wikipedia's listing, which had shown names and circumstances of individuals murdered by police, began to simply list the total numbers by month and a final tally based on all the month's totals. Clicking on the month would then take you to a page where each person's name and the circumstances of their murder by police would be listed, if known.

FBI statistics on the numbers of people killed by police is all but non-exist. "Justifiable Homicide," the label under which police murder is camouflaged, is not considered a crime. Neither officer-involved shootings nor "justifiable homicide" statistics from law enforcement agencies are required by the FBI.

Subsequent to the February, 2012, murder of 17-year old Trayvon Martin by George Zimmerman in Sanford, Florida, the Malcolm X Grassroots Movement authored two reports: "No More Trayvons: Every 36 Hours" and an updated "We Charge Genocide: Every 28 Hours," which documents the numbers of Black men, women and children who have been murdered by law enforcement, security guards, and white vigilantes extra-judicially, meaning, without due process, arrest, trial, sentencing – simply executed. The report roughly found that one person of Afrikan descent was murdered every one-to-one-and-a-half days but it only documents the year 2012. For that year a total 313 Black men, women and children lost their lives to police/state-sanctioned murder according to the report.

But that is only one year.

Suffice to say, the numbers of all people murdered by the police far, far outnumber the numbers of police officers who are killed in the line of duty. And the numbers of those who are of Afrikan descent killed by law enforcement is even more skewed. Murder by police is at crisis levels in the United States. And because it is state-sanctioned violence, the police continue to get away with it.

Black–on–Black violence which results in the loss of life also has its genesis in state violence. It is government, not in terms of Democrats or Republicans, Conservatives or Liberals, but the white supremacist state that has 1) enforced 'responsible' policing and crime control in white communities, 2) actually relocated crime to Black communities, while it 3) showed indifference to the conditions it created in Black communities at the same time responding to the issues of poverty, vice and crime in white communities, says Khalil Gibran Muhammad.

The white supremacist state has openly engaged in criminal activity in Black communities through programs such as Iran-Contra, flooding Black communities with guns and drugs, and actively encouraging and watching Blacks kill Blacks over drug money and gold chains. Leniency in policing and sentencing when Blacks commit crimes against one another, as well as miseducation and inferiorization and self-hate have inculcated a belief that money, gold chains, tennis shoes and other trinkets are more valuable than Black life within many of our communities. Black-on-Black violence is lateral violence: it is the striking out at those closest to you instead of the one who is causing your oppression, and it is absolutely encouraged by a white supremacist state, but it is still illegal and nine times out of ten, the perpetrators are arrested, convicted and sent to prison.

The responses to both state violence and the "lateral violence" of Blacks striking out at each other usually follow the same path: appeals are made to both elected bodies and the guilty parties (police) for condemnation and investigation; funding is sought to provide jobs for Black communities, even though both unemployed and gainfully employed Blacks commit murders and are murdered by the state; there is internal, grassroots community intervention - organizing aimed at raising awareness and mobilizing large numbers of people; as well as intra-racial appeals which are reminiscent of the late 19th and early 20th centuries calls for a "Talented Tenth" and "racial uplift." Responses to police murders in particular include protests, marches and rallies on police stations, headquarters and commissions, demanding that murdering police officers are fired, investigated, charged and jailed. But this approach rarely results in the type of justice that Black people are yearning for: an indication from the white supremacist state that Black lives matter and are valued by finding the offending officers guilty and jailing them. This yearning is a contradiction on its face. It is also a back-end solution.

A front-end solution to the crisis of police murder must be to confront the state and its front-line soldiers: the police. This confrontation can occur in several ways.

Public policy is one way however that can be a long and arduous process in which many more Black lives will undoubtedly be lost before victory is achieved. But in going the public policy route we must endeavor to do it differently than it has been traditionally accomplished. Media and policy analyst and organizer Makani Themba explains why:

> We often labor under the mistaken assumption that law is created by case history and argued in courts. As a result, the bulk of resources targeted for racial justice work are invested in groups engaged in legal defense strategies. Yet, law is so much more than cases. Law is a fluid amalgamation of **principle** – ideals like freedom, liberty, equality; **public perception and meaning** – how we come to understand what principles mean in our current context; **code** – the nitty-gritty words and technicalities that make up how these principles are implemented to and for whom; **coercion and intimidation** – we follow laws that don't work for us because we'd rather not deal with the consequences. [Emphasis in original].
>
> The Right understands the importance of *all* these elements in the forging of law and social norms. They push for

cases that push us on all these fronts; they work to control not only the public narrative but the institutions that shape meaning and teach us what to think about the world and each other; *and they defend vigilante and state violence that works to limit our freedom, our mobility and even our dreams of what's possible for our children. Trying to counter these efforts with law centered strategy is like expecting to beat a card shark at poker – using their marked deck.* [Emphasis mine].

In addition to public policy, we should also keep the option of armed self-defense as a valid response to the crisis of white supremacist state-sanctioned violence on the table. Armed self-defense is an alarming idea to some but it is not a new idea. Ida B. Wells-Barnett, Robert Charles, the Afrikan Blood Brotherhood, Robert and Mabel Williams, the Deacons for Defense, The Black Panther Party for Self-Defense, the Provisional Government of the Republic of New Afrika, June Jordan, Sagon Penn, Larry Davis, Terrance Johnson, Tupac Amaru Shakur, and numerous others in our history have all either advocated or practiced armed self-defense against white supremacist terror, be it in the form of individuals, organizations or the police, at one time or another.

The 20th Century's most well known proponent of armed self-defense, Malcolm X, leveled his charges squarely at both government and the police, saying that Black people should form rifle clubs and that Black people also

> "...should have the right to defend themselves against any attack made against them by anyone. If a dog is biting a black man the black man should kill the dog, *whether the dog is a police dog*, a hound dog or any kind of dog. If a dog is sicced on a black man when that black man is doing nothing but trying to take advantage of what the government says is supposed to be his then that black man should kill that dog or any two-legged dog who sics the dog on him." (Berkeley, 1963) [Emphasis mine].

Malcolm X was of course referring to the unleashing of police dogs on Civil Rights protestors in Birmingham, Alabama. The protesters were breaking segregation laws which is why the police used the dogs against them. Malcolm X considered the laws to be unjust, thus his admonishment.

Even the poet June Jordan was moved to

comment on the relevance of armed self-defense by Black people. In her work "Poem About Police Violence," Jordan asked a very simple question:

Tell me something
What you think would happen if
Everytime they kill a black boy
Then we kill a cop
Everytime they kill a black man
Then we kill a cop
You think the accident rate would lower
subsequently?

Jordan references the police murder of businessman Arthur McDuffie in Miami in 1980 in her poem and notes how the claim of an "accidental shooting" is a frequent one:

People been having accidents all over the
globe
So long like that I reckon that the only
Suitable insurance is a gun
I'm saying war is not to understand or rerun
War is to be fought and won

Jordan's poem is an example of what would be considered illegal self-defense in that it is retaliatory. In California, people have the legal right to resist an unlawful arrest; People v. White (1980) held that "An unlawful arrest includes both an arrest made without legal grounds and an arrest made with excessive force." Many of the interactions between police and Black/Brown people, particularly males, exceed "excessive force" and border on attempted murder. Even Florida v. Royer held that "when an officer, without reasonable suspicion or probable cause, approaches an individual, the individual has a right to ignore the police and go about his business." Such a scenario would, of course, undoubtedly cause a police officer to act more aggressive towards the person, which would thereby increase the need for lawful self-defense.

In 2012, the state of Indiana amended a 2006 bill that allowed for the use of force by an individual to "protect the person or a third person from what the person reasonably believes to be the imminent use of unlawful force." This bill was amended with the inclusion of the term "public servant." The term was added after a 2011 Supreme Court ruling held that people did not have the right to "reasonably resist unlawful entry by police officers," or "the imminent use of unlawful force." Now they do.

Over the last few years the police murder of loved ones has created politically active individuals and families, many of whom had heretofore not been active in their communities. If there is a silver lining to the unjust murder of their loved ones by police this might be it, although it is of course tainted by the very murders that were committed. Many of these same families of police murder victims have created non-profit entities to institutionalize their work, which is also a good thing. However, few if any of them have as their stated or implied mission the confronting of the very murderers of their loved ones: the police. A movement to confront the state-sanctioned murder of Black people by police is what is needed. This movement can be lead by the families of police murder victims or not, but a movement it must be. This is no longer debatable.

Armed self-defense against state-sanctioned violence is a legitimate and necessary response; as legitimate and necessary as voting and petition-gathering. Regardless of this truth however, it will not matter if we focus on public policy, the legal arena, armed self-defense, or a combination of all these tactics to bring an end to the state-sanctioned murder of Black people if we don't do some basic activism and organizing. That basic activism and organizing will not bear fruit unless we (re)create a sense of consciousness and a sense of community amongst ourselves as Black people.

We must begin to care for one another as members of a group with a similar ancestry, history and destiny. As part of this, we should proactively study and utilize non-violent, restorative justice principles for the internal conflicts and antagonisms that exist in our homes, on our blocks, in our communities, in every city we reside in. This can also slow the tide of Black–on–Black violence, a phenomenon that has its roots in white supremacist violence against Black people, but a phenomenon that is also used as a red herring against Black people when we rightfully condemn state-sanctioned, white supremacist murder.

This consciousness and this sense of community that must be nurtured amongst us must in turn be supplemented by concrete solidarity by our allies. That means all those justice-loving people who understand that white supremacy, while focusing on Afrikan-descended people specifically, is detrimental to all communities, all countries, and the planet that we all inhabit. This is a minimum of what is needed in order to reach a critical mass of people who are committed to ending the state-sanctioned murder of Black people.

I have already seen a glimpse of this consciousness, this sense of community and this solidarity. I saw it as a small piece of beauty in the ugly murder of Oscar Grant by Johannes Mehserle and Tony Pirone. That beauty was a vast ocean of allies – people of varying identities, ethnicities, cultures, genders, sexualities – who were as horrified and angered over the murder of Oscar Grant as Black people were; people who were just as insulted by Mehserle's taser lie as Black people were; and people who took to the streets with us to demand that Mehserle be held accountable for his crime. This ocean was simply *beautiful*.

I am thankful to have had the opportunity to observe this trial and report back to my community. I am also thankful to have observed first-hand some of the movement in the streets which made this trial possible in the first place. I have offered this book, this documentation, as my small contribution to that vast and beautiful ocean.

This is my witnessing.

This is my story.

And I'm sticking to it.

Thandisizwe Chimurenga
Los Angeles, CA
February, 2014

WORKS CITED

Abraham, Zennie. "Oakland City Attorney John Russo on Marijuana, Oscar Grant, World Cup Soccer." *City Brights* Blog, blog.sfgate.com/abraham, June 4, 2010.

Alexander, Michelle. *The New Jim Crow: Mass Incarceration in the Age of Colorblindness.* New York: The New Press, 2010.

Antony, Mary Grace and Thomas, Ryan J. "This is Citizen Journalism at its Finest: YouTube and the Public Sphere in the Oscar Grant Shooting Incident," *New Media and Society* 12 (8): 1280-1296 (2010).

Batson v. Kentucky, 476 U.S. 79, 1986.

Bell, Derrick. "Police Brutality: Portent of Disaster and Discomforting Divergence," in Nelson, Jill, *Police Brutality: An Anthology.* New York: W.W. Norton and Company, 2001.

Bugliosi, Vincent. *The Betrayal of America: How the Supreme Court Undermined the Constitution and Chose Our President.* New York: Nation Books, 2001.

Bulwa, Demian. "BART officer has yet to give account in shooting," *San Francisco Chronicle*, January 6, 2009.

Bulwa, Demian. "Oscar Grant's Character, Shooter Both on Trial." *San Francisco Chronicle*, May 30, 2010

Burns, Sarah. *The Central Park Five: The Untold Story Behind One of New York City's Most Infamous Crimes.* New York: Anchor Books/Random House 2012.

Cabaniss, Mark. "The Fullerton Six: A Death Penalty Case," www.fullertonsfuture.org, Sept. 8, 2011.

Cabaniss, Mark. "OC DA's Policy Of Pre-emptive Surrender," www.calwatchdog.com, Sept. 12, 2011.

California Department of Corrections and Rehabilitation, "Time Served on Prison Sentence: Felons First Released to Parole by Offense, Calendar Year 2009. Sacramento: March 2010.

Davis, Angela. *Are Prisons Obsolete?* San Francisco: Open Media Series/City Lights Publishing, 2003.

Dred Scott v. John F.A. Sanford, March 6, 1857; Case Files 1792-1995; Record Group 267; Records of the Supreme Court of the United States; National Archives.

DuBois, W.E.B. *Black Reconstruction in America: 1860-1880.* The Free Press/Simon and Schuster. New York: 1962.

Egelko, Bob. "Brown pushes D.A. to act swiftly in BART case," *San Francisco Chronicle*, Jan. 11, 2009

Florida v. Royer, 460 U.S. 491, (1983)

Hing, Julianne. "Johannes Mehserle Speaks," October 29, 2010. www.colorlines.com

hooks, bell. *Killing Rage Ending Racism.* Henry Holt and Company.New York: 1995

Jordan, June. "Poem About Police Violence." *Directed by Desire. The Collected Poems of June Jordan. Port Townsend:* Copper Canyon Press, 2005.

Kelley, Robin D.G. "The U.S. v. Trayvon Martin: How the System Worked," July 15, 2013, www.huffingtonpost.com

Kly, Y.N. *The Anti-Social Contract.* Clarity Press: Atlanta, 1989.

Meyer, Greg. "The Gap": How loss of the neck restraints led to the Rodney King incident," Jan. 19, 2007, www.policeone.com

Mills, Charles. *The Racial Contract*. Ithaca: Cornell University Press, 1999.

Mindich, David. *Just The Facts: How 'Objectivity' Came To Define American Journalism*. New York: New York, University Press, 1998.

Muhammad, Khalil Gibran. *The Condemnation of Blackness: Race, Crime, and the Making of Modern Urban America*. Cambridge: Harvard University Press, 2011.

Nelson, Jill. Introduction, *Police Brutality: An Anthology*. New York: W.W. Norton and Company, 2001.

Niquette, Mark. "NRA-Backed Law Spells Out When Indianans May Open Fire on Police," June 4, 2012, **www.bloomberg.com**.

People v. Johannes Mehserle. US. Los Angeles County Superior Court. 2010 (transcripts, motions, minute orders).

People v. Johannes Mehserle. US. Alameda County Superior Court. 2009 (transcripts, motions).

Sen, Rinku. "Applied Research Center's Strategic Framework for Advancing Racial Justice," January 2009, www.hazenfoundation.org

People v. White, 1980, 101 Cal App.3d, p.167. US. California Court of Appeals, 4th District.

People v. Wilkins, 2011, G040716, US. California Court of Appeals

Smith, Andrea. "Heteropatriarchy and the Three Pillars of White Supremacy: Rethinking Women of Color Organizing." *The Color Violence: the Incite! Anthology*. Boston: South End Press, 2006.

Smith, Matt, "Legal Weapon: Don Cameron trains cops in how to use force, and then defends them in court when

they're accused of going too far," *San Francisco Weekly*, Feb 10, 2010.

Themba, Makani. "Beyond Case Justice: Reimagining remedies for the 21st Century in the wake of the Zimmerman verdict," July 15, 2013, www.thepraxisproject.org.

Williams, Kristian. *Our Enemies in Blue: Police and Power in America*. Boston: South End Press, 2007.

Williams, Lance. "Ex-BART cop got big break at sentencing, records show," December 2, 2010, **www.californiawatch.com**.

Wright, Bobby. *The Psychopathic Racial Personality and Other Essays*. Chicago: Third World Press, 1985.

I N D E X

Kidnappings, 36
*Killing Rage Ending
Racism. See bell hooks*
King, Rodney, 52, 96, 196
Kivel, Paul, 33
Kly, Dr. Y. N., 171-172, 196
Knudtson, Emery, 9, 22
KTVU, 10, 11, 88-89

L.A. Confidential, 135
Lewelling Bl., 49
Libel: of Oscar Grant, 57, 81, 86-87
Liu, Daniel, 9, 19-20, 26, 29, 55
Los Angeles: County Jail, 5, 11, 149
Lynching, 89

Malice: aforethought, express, implied, 109-110
Manslaughter, 8, 113
Manslaughter: Involuntary, 5, 11, 89, 99-100, 113-114, 133, 148-150, 164; Voluntary, 113, 149
Manson, Charles, 151
Martin, Trayvon, 8, 136, 183, 196
Mastagni, David, 9, 59-61
Mayhem, 111-112, 121
McDuffie, Arthur, 189
Media: as cheerleader, 8
Mehserle, Johannes 5-11,

21-31, 33-36, 38-39, 41-42, 44, 52-62, 63-78, 81-82, 84, 86-90, 92, 94, 96, 99-104, 108, 110-111, 113-115, 117-121, 123-124, 126-129, 133, 135-136, 138-141, 143, -152, 155,-156, 158-161, 163-164, 167, 171, 192, 196-197
Mehserle, Todd (father of Johannes Mehserle), 102-104
Mesa, Sophina, 9, 13, 15-16, 22, 179, 208
Meyer, Greg, 9, 51-52, 115-116, 196
Mills, Charles, 167-168, 172, 197
Minimization, 33, 38
Mindich, David, 89, 197
Morality. *See* The 5 Promises
Most Huggable *See Johannes Mehserle*
Motion in Limine to Admit Breath Alcohol Form See BAT
Movement, Malcolm X Grassroots, 183
Muhammad, Khalil Gibran, 170, 184, 197
Murder, 5-8, 34, 59, 81-82, 88-89, 109-115, 121, 123, 125-126, 129, 133, 135, 140-141, 145, 149,

ACKNOWLEDGEMENTS

I am forever indebted to both Oakland, CA-based journalist JR Valrey for telling me to give Kevin Weston a call when I was looking for freelance gigs, and to Kevin Weston who approached Sandy Close and New America Media; Susan Mernit and Oakland Local; David Cohn and Spot.Us; and Mary Ratcliff and the San Francisco BayView newspaper to hire me to cover Johannes Mehserle's murder trial.

I solicited and received critical feedback on the manuscript for this book from several individuals, even hunting some of them down when they didn't get back to me quickly enough. In the end however, I made the decision to write this book in the way that I felt most comfortable. I own all mistakes and screw-ups in telling this aspect of Oscar's story and I sincerely appreciate the time these folks took to read my work and share their honest thoughts with me: Phyllis Jackson; Bruce Dixon; Jared Ball; Sikivu Hutchinson; Laura Whitehorn; Jill Nelson; Kay Kersplebedeb; James Simmons; Caro Gomez; Hala Dillsi; Kali Akuno and Monique Matthews.

Many, many, many thanks go to Jennifer Bihm for her critical eye and her helpful hand; to attorneys James Simmons and Nana Gyamfi who provided more free legal consultation than should be acknowledged in print; and to Robin Ritchie Casanova for fitting a sista into her morning routine and getting me to that courthouse every day.

I am especially thankful to Oscar's mom Wanda Johnson and uncle Cephus Johnson and Jack Bryson, Sr., for their assistance. I pray that their families, in addition to Oscar's friends who were with him that night – Carlos Reyes, Jackie Bryson, Nigel Bryson, Michael Greer, Fernando Anicette, Jamil Dewar, Chris Rafferty and the family of Johntue Caldwell (as well as Sophina Mesa and Tatiana Mesa Grant) – are granted justice and are able to heal from the unjust trauma they were subjected to.

Many Thanks and Much Love to my Family – My Ancestors, named and unnamed, known and unknown, as well as the Living – for all of the ways that Family holds you and comes to your rescue when you need them: my mother and father Annise and Neal Decree; my grandparents Benny and Minnie, Derry and Fannie – Mojuba, Ibase Egun, Ibae Bae Tonu; my siblings, nieces, nephew and cousins: Jennifer, Lee, Darryl, Miriam, LeAmber, Renee and Alex, Rudy Wesley, "Lil" Anthony Horton and "Big" Lou Brown.

There were many, many folks who helped me get through the writing process of this book. A few of them don't have the first clue that they provided assistance but words of encouragement and inspiration; a listening ear for a rant or a vent; returning phone calls and e-mails and phone calls and returning phone calls; raucous laughter; free food; free money; some distractions, and unconditional love played a potent and necessary part in getting this book to fruition. Therefore, I must, with all of my heart, say Asante Sana, Medase Paa, Modupe Pupo –

Thank You Very Much – to the following:

Friends, Comrades, and Counselors: Orunmila Eleri Ipin, Esu Odara, Iyanifa Fayomi F. A. Obafemi; Monique Matthews; Akua Ofeibea Abotare; Kwame Afari; Shaunelle Curry; Zak Kondo; Karin Stanford; Queen Sy; Talibah Shakir; Afia Khalia; Jasmin Young; Malcolm Harris; Tatyanna Wilkinson; Nwabueze Brooks; Tamika Miller; Bilal Ali; Khanum Shaikh; Deborah Hailu; Erebka Henry; Kymberly Newberry; Kokayi kwa Jitahidi; Akua Jitahadi; Aquil Basheer; Nandi Sojourner Crosby; Emani Dawson-Bey; Rasheed Shabazz; Sally Hampton; Desiree Bizzell; Zenzele Tanya Bell; Oyatunde Amakisi; Semba Love; Shoshana Vogel; Patrice Cullors Brignac; Sharifa Johka; Mark Anthony Johnson; Dranae Jones; Chico Norwood; Brad Pye, Jr.; The 8-Ball Foundation; Sara Harris; Melissa Chiprin; Kali Akuno; Kofi Shakur; William Campbell; Jahsun Edmonds; David Dang; Tiffany Wallace; Julia Wallace; Sam Sunshine; Linguere Sheba Lo; Jenn Kluu; Delesha Trim; Leslie Radford; Kellie Hawkins; Ryan Thompson; Muneera Shariff Gardezi and Sameer Asad Gardezi; Carmen Dixon Rosenzweig; Christabel Nsiah-Buadi; Joanne Griffith Poplar; Mari Tyner; Nancy Lockhart; and all the members of the Los Angeles Coalition for Justice for Oscar Grant including Tiah Starr, Aidge Patterson, Hala Dillsi, Caro Gomez, Kelley del Gado, Elizabeth Venable and Jubilee Shine.

Thank you to the wonderful Yemi Toure for simply being.

A Super Duper, Double O Soul Shout Out goes to W. Paul Coates of Black Classic Press, Lawrence

Grandpre, and Dominique Stevenson, Dominique Stevenson, and DOMINIQUE STEVENSON!

I am grateful to the journalists and media workers who interviewed me during and after the trial or reprinted some of my articles: Kevin Weston; Davey D, Anita Johnson and Hard Knock Radio; JR Valrey and Block Report Radio; Sabrina Jacobs and the Morning Mix; Mary Ratcliff and the San Francisco Bay View Newspaper; Rasheed Shabazz; Jesse Strauss; Charlene Muhammad; Esther Armah and Wake Up Call; Imhotep Gary Byrd and the Global Black Experience; Dedon Kamathi and Freedom Now Radio; Sonali Kolhatkar and Uprising; Michael Datcher, Kimberly Perry and Beautiful Struggle Radio; Eric Mann and Voices from the Frontlines Radio; Donna Wallach and Free Our Minds Radio; Ewuare Osayande; Bruce Dixon; Jared Ball; Ernesto Aguilar, and Kevin Alexander Gray.

I am greatly indebted to Sikivu Hutchinson for selflessly sharing her knowledge of self-publishing and ePublishing with me.

Many thanks to court stenographers Beth Quintana and Phyllis Lee, who were wonderful, gracious and speedy on the turnaround; and Elizabeth "Liz" Martinez, L.A. County Superior Court Public Information Officer, for her patience, helpfulness and pleasant demeanor.

Five individuals that I simply *must* single out:

Sheena Chou used all of her graphics skills and

all of her graphics powers with many of the photos for this book, including the cover photo. This was facilitated through late, late night phone call and e-mail bombardments and for that I will be eternally grateful.

Myshell Tabu designed the fabulous cover and formatted the eBook and did a whole buncha other things on short notice while skillfully juggling wifely-mommy-homeschooling-SistaFriend-and-other duties, along with e-mail and text message bombardments with class, style and a sense of humor. She was most merciful and I am so thankful to her.

Not long after I found out I would be covering the trial, I mentioned it to **Carmen Morgan** and the first words out of her mouth were "Oh Thandi … that's a book!" She was serious too. My mind was unable to fully process her words at the time, so I simply filed them away. I eventually stopped apologizing *to her* for not beginning right then and there the process of writing, once I understood that this book was birthed when it decided it was ready to be born. Thank you, Carmen, for the spark and for genuinely, purposefully modeling support in concrete, practical ways.

Phyllis Jackson has been a tremendous source of clarity and inspiration throughout the entire process of this book, graciously indulging hours-long phone calls, helping me excavate the depths of white supremacy and walking me through the various ways that it maintains its murderous self. Thanks to her, eyes that I thought were already wide open have truly been enlarged even further. I am deeply and humbly appreciative for her presence in my life.

I am convinced that **David Morse (Dave Id)** of the San Francisco Bay Independent Media Center was sent to me (all of these people were sent to me, but Dave was *really, really* sent specifically *to me*). Dave's desire to archive as much material as possible about the trial made him my natural ally and he graciously facilitated the process of securing the transcripts and videos that were entered into evidence at Johannes Mehserle's criminal trial in Los Angeles. I am so grateful to and appreciative for him I almost don't know what to say, other than 1) a really really great, big, huge, gigantic, enormous, ginormous THANK YOU! 2) I also want to urge you to support the preservation of the Justice for Oscar Grant News Archive at indybay.org/oscargrant, and 3) support independent media in general, *but only if it supports you and your concerns.*

Finally, I extend a heartfelt Thank You to the Army of Healers and Conjurers who soothed my soul during the re-telling of Oscar's murder(s). They pulled me through the entire process of writing this book and for that I am most grateful: Phyllis Hyman; Stevie Wonder; The Isley Brothers; DJ Osunlade; DJ Lynnee Denise; Rose Royce; Lauren Hill; Thievery Corporation; Teena Marie; John Coltrane; Erykah Badu; The Spinners; Nina Simone; The Roots; En Vogue; Lupe Fiasco; the Mary Jane Girls; Billie Holiday; A Tribe Called Quest; Marvin Gaye; Coldplay; Mary J. Blige; Antibalas; Digable Planets; Tears for Fears; Robert Glasper; The Commodores;

Bessie Smith; El Chicano; Esperanza Spaulding; Heavy D and the Boys; Culture Club; Dinah Washington; The Stylistics; Jimmie Bo Horne; Charlie Parker; Jocelyn Brown and NuYoRican Soul; Tomandandy; De La Soul; Sara Vaughn; Malcolm MacClaren; Marlena Shaw; Blue States; Enchantment; Ella Fitzgerald; Flying Lotus; Harold Melvin and the Blue Notes; Dwight Trible; Hall and Oates, Angelique Kidjo; SOS Band; The Chacachas; Imani Uzuri; Afia Khalia; Esther Phillips; the RZA; Sage Francis; Gaelle; Christian Prommer; Pete Rock and CL Smooth; Pharoah Sanders; Meshell Ndegeocello; Jimmie Scott and John Beltran; Sade; Janelle Monae', Tracy Chapman and Gregory Porter.

ABOUT THE AUTHOR

Thandisizwe Chimurenga is an award-winning, grassroots freelance journalist based in Los Angeles, CA. She has been an activist, a writer and creator or co-creator of media (newspapers, cable tv and radio shows) for over 20 years, and her community activism has ranged from electoral organizing; anti-police terror work; freedom for political prisoners and prisoners of war, to organizing against violence against women. No Doubt: The Murder(s) of Oscar Grant is her first book. Author photo by *Guerrilla Queenz*.

The Ida B. Wells Institute
seeks to utilize
old and new forms of media
to
Advocate
Educate
and
Mobilize